Russia's
Military Aircraft
in the 21st Century

Yefim Gordon

Original translation by Dmitriy and Sergey Komissarov

MIDLAND

An imprint of
Ian Allan Publishing

Russia's Military Aircraft in the 21st Century
© 2006 Yefim Gordon

ISBN (10) 1 85780 224 1
ISBN (13) 978 1 85780 224 5

Published by Midland Publishing
4 Watling Drive, Hinckley, LE10 3EY, England
Tel: 01455 254 490 Fax: 01455 254 495
E-mail: midlandbooks@compuserve.com

Midland Publishing is an imprint of
Ian Allan Publishing Ltd

Worldwide distribution (except North America):
Midland Counties Publications
4 Watling Drive, Hinckley, LE10 3EY, England
Telephone: 01455 254 450   Fax: 01455 233 737
E-mail: midlandbooks@compuserve.com
www.midlandcountiessuperstore.com

North American trade distribution:
Specialty Press Publishers & Wholesalers Inc.
39966 Grand Avenue, North Branch, MN 55056, USA
Tel: 651 277 1400   Fax: 651 277 1203
Toll free telephone: 800 895 4585
www.specialtypress.com

Design concept and layout by
Polygon Press Ltd (Moscow, Russia)

This book is illustrated with photos by Yefim Gordon,
Sergey Krivchikov, Sergey Sergeyev, Aleksandr
Drobyshevskiy, Vladimir Drobyshevskiy, Victor
Drushlyakov, Sergey Balakleyev, Vyacheslav
Martyniuk, Sergey Pashkovskiy, Pavel Novikov,
the late Sergey Skrynnikov, and from the archives
of the Sukhoi Holding Co., Rostvertol Plant, the
Ulan-Ude Aircraft Factory, *Vertolyot* magazine, Yefim
Gordon, and the Russian Aviation Research Trust.
Line drawings by RSK MiG and Yakovlev Corp.

Printed in England by Ian Allan Printing Ltd
Riverdene Business Park, Molesey Road,
Hersham, Surrey, KT12 4RG

Visit the Ian Allan Publishing website at:
www.ianallanpublishing.com

Contents

Title page: The Su-27KUB shipboard trainer prototype, '21 Blue', in camouflage colours at a late stage of the test programme.
This page: '156 White', the MiG-29M2 prototype, makes a tight turn over the control tower at Zhukovskiy with Pavel Vlasov at the controls during the MAKS-2005 airshow. Note the smoke generator pods which many would be sorely tempted to call 'Smokewinders'.

Front cover: '01 White', the first Yak-130 trainer in representative production configuration, pictured in a test flight.
Rear cover, top: Su-27SM '80 Red' at Komsomol'sk-on-Amur/Dzemgi; bottom: Mi-24PN '58 Red' performs at the Flying Legends-2005 airshow.

Introduction

Fifteen years before the turn of the century, sweeping political changes known as *perestroika* ('restructuring') began in the Soviet Union. The end result was obviously not what the authors of the new policy had intended: in 1991 the Soviet Union ceased to exist, disintegrating into 15 new nations. Most of the former Soviet republics then formed a loose confederation called the Commonwealth of Independent States (CIS). Of all the CIS states, the Russian Federation was by far the biggest and had the most powerful industrial amd military structure.

Of course, Russia in general and its Armed Forces were hard hit by the economic crisis of the 1990s. Among other things, huge reductions were made in the Air Force, hundreds of aircraft being placed in storage, sold abroad or scrapped due to service life limits, obsolescence or unit disbandment caused by defence cuts. As the state defence orderbook (and civil orders) shrank to almost nothing, the Russian aircraft industry came to a halt, surviving only thanks to the few export contracts that were secured.

The prospects for the Russian economy and the Armed Forces started improving when Vladimir V. Putin was elected President in 2000. A new Russian military doctrine was proclaimed, the defence policy priorities were redefined, and a government programme to create a new model army capable of meeting the challenges of the time was adopted.

In the 1990s the combat readiness of the Russian Air Force was put to the test both in actual warfare (the two Chechen wars) and in various all-arms and tactical exercises. The current viewpoint prevailing in Russia is that in present-day conditions and the nearest future Russia's military security cannot be safeguarded without a mighty Air Force formed by uniting the originally separate Air Force (VVS – *Voyenno-voz**dooshnyye* **see***ly*) and Air Defence Force (PVO – ***Pro**tivovoz**doosh**naya obo**ron**a*). This is especially true in the case of large-scale conventional (non-nuclear) warfare. This is a fact which has been proved more than once in the armed conflicts of the 20th century.

Effective air support of the ground forces is one of the key components of success in any kind of combat operations, be it defence or offensive/counteroffensive actions This holds true for both major wars and local conflicts. The Russian Air Force has played a key role in the destruction of Chechen guerrilla strongholds, command posts, anti-aircraft assets and armoured vehicles during the first Chechen War (1994-96) and Second Chechen War (1999-2001). The present-day Russian Air Force formed by the 'merger' of the VVS and the PVO is fulfilling a strategic task of national importance – the reliable protection of political/administrative and defence industry centres, communications centres, the nation's top military and political command, the assets of Russia's United Energy System (power stations, high-voltage lines and so on) and other important infrastructure against air strikes and attacks from outer space (that is, ballistic missile strikes or attack from Earth orbit) by any aggressor.

Obviously this cannot be done without state-of-the-art combat aircraft. Hence lately the Russian government has been committing considerable resources to the task of rebuilding the nation's defence industry in the new market economy conditions and supplying the national aircraft and defence industry with orders for the home market. (Export orders are all very well, – the export potential of Russian military hardware is well-known, – but the Russian Air Force's aircraft fleet is in need of renewal and/or upgrading.) Funds have been allocated for mid-life updates (MLUs) of the fighters, bombers, attack aircraft and helicopters currently in service which, in the opin-

A line-up of 'hunchback' MiG-29s *sans suffixe* (*izdeliye* 9.13 or *Fulcrum-C*) at Kubinka airbase. The MiG-29 is one of the Russian Air Force's two principal fighter types and the fleet is due for an upgrade.

Above: An interesting formation of Tupolev strategic aircraft – a Tu-95MS missile carrier leading a Tu-160 missile carrier (left wingman) and a Tu-22M3 bomber/ missile carrier – at the MAKS-95 airshow in Zhukovskiy. All three types now form the mainstay of Russia's strategic aviation component.

ion of the Russian military, will allow these aircraft to remain in service for at least another ten years. Export contracts allow the leading Russian aircraft deign bureaux to continue development of new aircraft types and the resulting refinements can be incorporated on the Russian Air Force's aircraft as well. Among other things, the government's list of priorities for the defence industry includes development of a fifth-generation fighter provisionally known as PAK FA (*perspektivnyy aviatsionnyy kompleks frontovoy aviahtsii* – Advanced Tactical Aviation Aircraft System), and the work is going on in high gear.

This book makes use of material published in the Russian press and informatioon released at various airshows and trade fairs, press conferences, briefings and roll-outs to give a brief account of current Russian military aviation programmes. A full account would require a much larger book to do these programmes justice. Nevertheless this book will give the reader an idea of the Russian Air Force's combat potential in the nearest future.

Below: The Sukhoi Su-27 is the other principal fighter type now operated in Russia. This example is equipped with Sorbtsiya ECM pods at the wingtips.

Chapter 1

Sukhoi's Programmes

Upgrading the Su-24M

The Sukhoi Su-24 *Fencer* 'swing-wing' tactical bomber, which is the main strike aircraft of the Russian Air Force's tactical arm (FA – *Frontovaya aviahtsiya*), underwent several upgrades back in the Soviet days.

One of the last 'radical' upgrades, known as the Su-24BM (*bol'shaya modernizahtsiya* – major upgrade), was proposed in the Sukhoi OKB in 1979. The proposal envisaged a substantial increase in the aircraft's dimensions; this entailed a considerable increase in the fuselage width, since a bomb bay was to be located between the engines (in contrast, the standard Su-24 carries all bombs and mis-

siles externally). The engines' inlet ducts were shortened (the air intakes were located under the wings in a manner similar to the General Dynamics F-111 Aardvark rather that just aft of the cockpit). However, the work on this machine was soon terminated: the customer (the Air Force) and the management of the aircraft industry gave preference to a more promising project representing the next generation of airborne combat systems (now known as the Su-27IB/Su-34 fighter-bomber).

Nevertheless, the OKB tried to resume the work on the Su-24BM. In particular, a project was offered visualising this machine as an air-

craft with fixed swept wings featuring leading-edge root extensions (LERXes), with twin vertical tails and a new avionics suite. The work went as far as the construction of a full-scale mock-up in 1983, but then the programme was terminated.

Two years later designers of the Sukhoi OKB studied different variants of the Su-24MM (*malaya modernizahtsiya* – minor upgrade) attack aircraft. The first of these variants featured a 2,000-kg (4,410-lb) increase of the all-up weight and increased range thanks to the installation of new, more powerful and fuel-efficient Lyul'ka AL-31F afterburn-

Su-24M '02 Red' (c/n 1041610) is seen at Akhtoobinsk on 27th September 2005 with a Kh-59MK air-to-surface missile (inert, judging by the orange-painted body) on the port wing glove pylon, a Kh-58 anti-radiation missile on the starboard wing glove pylon and two B-13L rocket pods on the swivelling outer wing pylons.

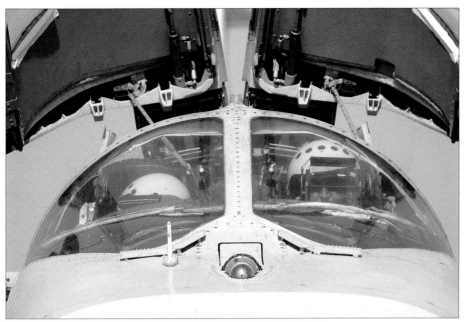

Above: The cockpit windshield of the Su-24M with the tip of the retracted in-flight refuelling (IFR) probe ahead of it. Note the head-up display at the pilot's station.

Above: Close-up of the Kh-59MK under the wing of Su-24M '02 Red', showing the plug closing the intake of the missile's engine before launch. Note the ventral BPK-9M pod housing guidance and test equipment.

This model of the upgraded Su-24M was displayed by Gefest & T at several Moscow airshows. Note the Kh-31 missiles on the wing glove pylons.

ing turbofans replacing the standard AL-21Fs. A distinctive feature of the new aircraft was an additional air intake above the fuselage to cater for the AL-31F engines' higher mass flow. The second variant, which was actively promoted by representatives of the Air Force, envisaged an increased range due to the use of conformal fuel tanks (this preceded the use of such tanks on the McDonnell Douglas F-15 Eagle in the USA). V. R. Kovtoon was one of the authors of the idea. However, the work on the Su-24MM did not proceed further than the initial design studies. Incidentally, wits deciphered the MM abbreviation as *Mertvorozhdennyy monstr* – Stillborn Monster – or as *Moo-Moo*, a mongrel dog from a story by Ivan S. Turgenev which was drowned at the order of a landlady – just like the Su-24MM 'was drowned' at the order of the higher powers.

Possibly the real reason was far more trivial – it was not some evil force from outside but the Sukhoi OKB itself that killed off the project. At that time the OKB had political reasons to promote the 'new-generation' Su-27IB/Su-34, despite the fact that, unlike the latter aircraft, the 'old' Su-24M had terrain-following capability (even at supersonic speeds) and was cheaper to operate than even the baseline Su-27 fighter, to say nothing of the more complex Su-27IB/Su-34.

In the 1990s the efforts to further refine the Su-24M were halted for a long time; the only exception was the integration of the Kh-31A anti-shipping missile and the Kh-31P anti-radiation missile, and then it was only a handful of *Fencer-Ds* that received this upgrade. A change of fortune came only at the end of the decade when the Russian Air Force and the Russian Naval Air Arm decided to keep the type in service at least until the end of 2010, whereupon the Su-24M was to be finally superseded by the Su-27IB (Su-34). However, the funding shortfalls that have become typical of modern Russia will undoubtedly delay the service entry of the latter aircraft. Besides, the Su-27IB will obviously complement the Su-24M rather than replace it completely; also, the air forces operating the Su-24MK export version are unlikely to find a replacement type before the end of 2010. That said, a mid-life update of the existing Su-24M/MK fleet concerned first and foremost with expanding the capabilities of the aircraft's avionics suite and integrating new weapons becomes of crucial importance.

Hence the Sukhoi Holding Co. has developed a number of Su-24M upgrade options ranging from the simple installation of a satellite navigation system receiver to a comprehensive update involving the installation of many avionics components from the latest Su-27IB. In the late 1990s the US Air Force retired its F-111 tactical bombers – the American counterpart of the Su-24. This was not

Above: Sporting the dark green/dark earth camouflage with pale blue undersides usually applied to export Su-24MKs, Su-24M2 '37 White outline' operated by the Russian Air Force's 929th State Flight Test Centre at Akhtoobinsk carries an inert Kh-31P ARM and a centreline guidance pod associated with it.

due to any performance shortfalls – indeed, the F-111 was the only American tactical aircraft capable of sustained ultra-low-level supersonic flight in automatic terrain-following mode; the decision was prompted by the high maintenance costs of the aircraft's outdated avionics and the apparent impossibility of a cost-effective upgrade.

This was taken into account by the design staff of the Gefest & T company which launched its own Su-24M upgrade programme in 1996. (*Gefest* is the Russian rendering of Hephaistos, the 'chief armourer' of Greek mythology.) Several other companies had similar programmes running; eventually, however, the Russian Air Force preferred the upgrade offered by Gefest & T over the competitors' proposals (including Sukhoi's) from a cost/effect standpoint. Gefest & T's Director A. N. Panin says only a fraction of the capabilities offered by third-generation avionics is used at present; weapons delivery is possible only within a small portion of the aircraft's flight envelope. Therefore the company's efforts were mostly directed at radically expanding the Su-24M's combat envelope (that is, the speed, altitude, bank angle and G load limits at which the weapons can be used) and pushing its limits towards the limits of the flight envelope. Introducing the ability to use the weapons during high-G manoeuvres is particularly important, since it reduces the risk

The Kh-31P belches flames after being released by Su-24M2 '37 White outline' during a test flight.

of being hit by the enemy's anti-aircraft fire and improves survivability.

Gefest & T has achieved a radical improvement of the Su-24M's combat efficiency by giving the upgraded bomber the ability to strike at ground and maritime targets while manoeuvring at will, be it in the daytime or at night and regardless of the weather; by increasing the navigation and targeting accuracy and automating the mission preparation

and post-mission analysis; and by expanding the range of weaponry. The upgrade involves replacing the Orbita-10-058 digital computer and the existing input/output device, both of which embody 1970s technology, with the state-of-the-art SV-24 specialised fast processor (*spetsializeerovannyy vychislitel'*) and the UVV-MP I/O device (*oostroystvo vvoda-vyvoda*). This improves the delivery accuracy of the unguided weapons while reducing the

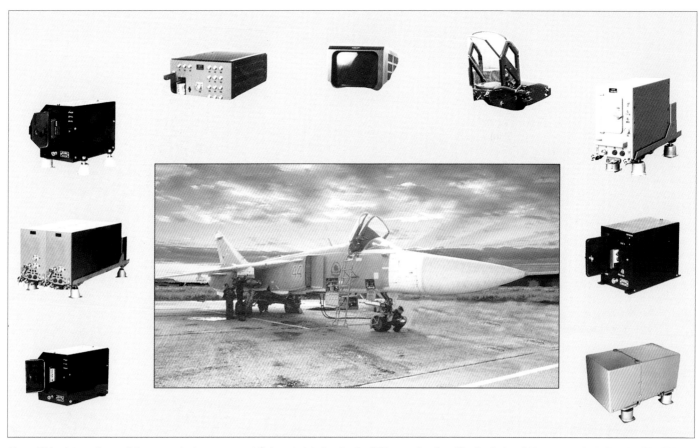

Above: This picture shows all the new avionics components integrated during the Su-24M upgrade offered by the Gefest & T company, including the OR4-TM display and the KAI-24P head-up display (top) and the ZTN-1 solid-state flight data recorder/cockpit voice recorder (right).

risk of being hit by anti-aircraft fire. Free-fall bombs released while manoeuvring at will in low-level flight can now be delivered with an accuracy comparable to that of guided bombs and placed on the target from a distance of 5-8 km (3-5 miles) without bringing the bomber within range of the target's anti-aircraft defence assets (AA artillery, Stinger and Igla man-portable air defence systems, Chaparral surface-to-air missiles and the like).

The addition of the Obzor-RBV-T radar signal processor (*obzor* = perspective, or field of view) and the state-of-the-art OR4-TM cathode-ray tube radar display, replacing the current OR4-T, facilitates target identification greatly. The Obzor-RBV-T digitally processes the radar imagery and converts it to TV format for presentation on the OR4-TM display. This update increases the identification range for targets with a high radar signature and improves radar rangefinding accuracy while offering higher resolution.

The OR4-TM display forming part of the radar data processing system can show the radar imagery superimposed on an electronic terrain map – for the first time in Russian practice. As a result, the capabilities of the upgraded Su-24M's navigation/attack suite featuring a simple centimetre-waveband radar approach the performance of a far more costly suite built around a synthetic aperture radar.

The crew finds it easier to locate and identify the designated target by watching the radar 'blips' superimposed on the map. Additionally, target updates can be uploaded to the aircraft in real time via datalink and displayed in graphical form against the background of the map. Moreover, the pilot can use the digital map (which can be enlarged to show even the runways of airfields located in the area) for navigation and landing approach in adverse weather. This significantly enhances the flexibility and rapid-reaction

The OR4-TM display installed at the WSO's workstation shows targets superimposed on a digital map; in this case it is a tank located 5.1 km (3.16 miles) away, with its precise coordinates given.

capability of tactical strike aviation and is an asset for combat aviation at large.

Another change in the cockpit of the upgraded aircraft is that the standard PPV head-up display (*pritsel'no-pilotazhnyy vizeer* – 'aiming/flying sight') gives way to the new KAI-24P HUD working with the BFI signal generator module. The new HUD provides the pilot with considerably more detailed information during navigation, attack and landing approach and facilitates contact with the tanker during in-flight refuelling. Additionally, the KAI-24 can display radar imagery combined with the electronic map as shown on the OR-4TM display.

The basic upgrade package offered by Gefest & T includes only modest changes to the cockpit data presentation and control systems; this is due not only to the wish to minimise the cost of the upgrade but also to the heightened pilot training requirements arising from a more extensive upgrade. Later, however, when pilots who have been trained from the outset to work with multi-function displays (MFDs) rimmed with command keys join the Air Force, such MFDs may be fitted to third-generation combat jets in the course of upgrades.

The installation of the SRNS-24 satellite navigation system receiver on the Su-24M allows the aircraft's coordinates to be determined with an error margin of a few metres. Working with the Russian GLONASS satellite system (*Globahl'naya navigatsionnaya spootnikovaya sistema*) and its US counterpart NAVSTAR, the SRNS-24 provides for the following:

Above: The logo of Gefest & T on the air intake trunk of '40 Red', one of the upgraded Su-24Ms operated by the Russian Air Force's 4th TsBP i PLS. Note the 'crosshairs' in the middle of the Cyrillic letter F.

Above: The same aircraft immediately after touching down at Lipetsk; note the open mainwheel well doors which double as airbrakes.

The landing run completed, Su-24M '40 Red' vacates the runway at Lipetsk, the twin cruciform brake parachutes billowing in the jet exhaust. Outwardly the examples upgraded by Gefest & T are almost indistinguishable from standard ones. Note the four mission markers aft of the cockpit.

Above: '44 Red', another Su-24M operated by the 4th TsBP i PLS, flies over the Central Russian countryside with 100-kg (220-lb) OFAB-100 bombs on all four wing pylons. It is seen here before the upgrade (note the lack of the Gefest & T logo on the air intakes visible on the photos on the next page).

The same aircraft drops a 250-kg (551-lb) FAB-500M-54 'dumb bomb' from the port outer wing pylon. Bombs are used sparingly during practice sorties. After the upgrade the aircraft acquired the ability to use precision-guided munitions.

Above: WIth access ladders propped up against the fuselage sides (not hooked up to the cockpit sills as they should be), '44 Red' awaits the next mission. An APA-5DM ground power unit based on a Ural-4320 6x6 lorry (Russian Army number plate 7038 vv [34]) supplies electric power to it and another Su-24M.

Melting the scenery behind it in the blast of its mighty Lyul'ka AL-21F-3 turbofans, Su-24M '44 Red' is waved off by a ground crewman as it taxies out for a training sortie. No bombs are carried this time.

Above: Flaps and leading-edge slats deployed, Su-24M '44 Red' passes a trio of Su-27 fighters resident at Lipetsk, two of which wear a non-standard colour scheme with Russian flag stripes across the tails and the top of the wings/centre fuselage. The Su-24's white radome tends to get very dirty over the years.

Yet another aspect of the same aircraft 'burning rubber' as it touches down at Savasleyka AB near Nizhniy Novgorod. The 3,000-litre (660 Imp gal) PTB-3000 drop tanks under the wing gloves reveal that the aircraft has come from afar on a positioning flight. Note the dorsal chaff/flare dispenser near the fin.

Above: Two FAB-250M-54 bombs on bomb lifts are ready for hooking up to Su-24M '45 Red' wearing the Sukhoi 'winged archer' logo, the Gefest & T logo, five mission markers and the image of a bull with the legend *Vsegda* (Always) – popularly explained as 'We'll have everybody, everywhere, always and in every way'!

'45 Red' starts up its engines with the ground power cables still attached; with no ear protection available, the technician crouching beside the aircraft has no choice but to plug his ears. The aircraft is armed with two S-24 heavy unguided rockets in this instance.

Above: Upgraded Su-24M lands at Savasleyka AB for a refuelling stop en route to Lipetsk as it returns from temporary deployment at a remote base. Note the open auxiliary blow-in door.

• determining the aircraft's current position, flight altitude above sea level and ground speed in autonomous and differential modes;

• determining the target's altitude above sea level (derived from information about the high points of the terrain being overflown);

• updating the computed coordinates, using the form field of the terrain being overflown;

• exchanging data with the SV-24 specialised processor.

The error margin during coordinate measurement is 15 m (49 ft) in autonomous mode and 3 m (10 ft) in differential mode; the error margin during altitude measurement in these modes is 25 m (82 ft) and 3 m respectively. The SRNS-24 weighs 3.2 kg (7.05 lb).

Changes are made to the data storage equipment. The MLP-14-3 tape recorder is replaced by the TBN-K-2 solid-state data storage module which saves the complete information supplied by the PNS-24M navigation/attack suite, the Tester flight data recording system and the Karpaty ECM suite on a single memory card of 64-100 Mb capacity. The 2T-3M (or 2TV) flight data recorder/cockpit voice recorder ('black box') forming part of the Tester-UZ system is replaced by the ZTN-1 crashworthy solid-state FDR/CVR (*zashchishchonnyy tverdotel'nyy nakopitel'*)

which is able to record the flight parameters at a rate of 256 words per second for up to 26 hours, record four voice communication channels for the last 30 minutes of the flight and save the results of the preceding ten missions' automatic analysis.

The new NKPiK mission preparation and post-flight analysis suite (*nazemnyy kompleks podgotovki i kontrolya*) makes the upgraded Su-24M a lot easier and cheaper to operate. The data recording systems capture information on the condition of the aircraft's systems, making it possible to determine what maintenance work, if any, is required. Currently Gefest & T is working on introducing built-in test equipment monitoring not only the avionics suite but airframe integrity as well.

A comparison of the standard Su-24M and the version upgraded by Gefest & T shows that the latter version offers the following advantages:

• conversion training is simple and the new equipment is easily mastered by the pilots and navigators/weapons systems operators;

• the flight/navigation and targeting information is adequate and presented in a convenient manner, significantly reducing the crew's psychological stress and physical workload and enabling the crew to work efficiently during daytime or night sorties;

• attacking the targets while manoeuvring at will is facilitated (this prevents tactical inflexibility which leads to higher own losses);

Four Su-24Ms of the 4th TsBP i PLS resting between missions at Lipetsk. Oddly, only one of them ('44 Red') has the additional upward-firing chaff/flare dispensers.

- the Su-24M bomber becomes simpler and easier to operate when attacking targets in the course of combined-arms operations;
- the operational mobility of the units equipped with the upgraded bombers increases by a factor of 2.2 and survivability is improved by 30-40%;
- the avionics' weight, size and power consumption are significantly reduced;
- day-to-day operation is simplified (the aircraft and the weapons system based on same can be operated on a 'technical condition' basis) and the average yearly operating costs are reduced by 17%;
- the aircraft can be upgraded on site within just five to seven days.

Three production Su-24Ms belonging to the Lipetsk-based 4th Combat & Conversion Training Centre (TsBP i PLS – *Tsentr boyevoy podgotovki i pereoochivaniya lyotnovo sostava*) named after Valeriy P. Chkalov were upgraded in this fashion in 1998, proving their new capabilities during routine training flights and various exercises. The latter included the *Roobezh-2004* (Frontier-2004) exercise held at a practice range in the mountains of Kyrghyzstan featuring fairly complicated terrain. Operating from Kant AB (a Russian Air Force base in Kyrghyzstan) where they were temporarily deployed for the occasion, the Su-24Ms destroyed a 'terrorist base camp' in accordance with the scenario of the exercise, earning the high appraisal of the defence ministers of the participating CIS republics. Over the past eight years the Su-24Ms upgraded by Gefest & T have proved their much-improved combat potential as compared to the standard aircraft. Similarly upgraded Su-24Ms with a slightly different avionics fit for export have been delivered to the Algerian Air Force (*Force Aérienne Algérienne/al Quwwat al-Jawwiya al'Jaza'eriya*); these are second-hand aircraft and the upgrade was performed by the Novosibirsk Aircraft Production Association (NAPO) which had built them, using Gefest & T technologies. Other nations have shown an interest in Su-24Ms thus upgraded.

The pilots and the command staff of the 4th TsBP i PLS operating the upgraded bombers are pleased as can be with their combat capabilities and maintainability. The only fly in the ointment is that the upgraded machines are all too few.

Actually there is another big fat fly in the ointment, but the Air Force is reluctant to talk about it. As already mentioned, the Sukhoi Holding Co. has developed its own upgrade programme known as the Su-24M2. A demonstrator coded '38 White' (c/n 1041643) has become a regular participant of the MAKS airshows in Zhukovskiy; another Su-24M2 coded '37 White outline' and likewise able to carry Kh-31 missiles was undergoing trials at the 929th State Flight Test Centre (GLITs – *Gosoodarstvennyy lyotno-ispytahtel'nyy tsentr*) at Vladimirovka AB, Akhtoobinsk. Many Russian aerospace industry and defence experts hold the view that the efforts to modernise the Russian Air Force's and the Russian Navy's *Fencer-D* fleets are being scuttled mainly by Sukhoi's desire to get the Russian MoD to select the company's upgrade programme over the competitors' bids or, better still, to further the service entry of the more advanced Su-27IB/Su-34 strike aircraft.

On its part, the Sukhoi Holding Co. believes that the avionics should not be the only area to receive attention during an upgrade of the Su-24M. Drawing on the experience of tactical strike aircraft utilisation in the local wars of the last decade, Sukhoi designers have given much attention to increasing the bomber's survivability. This includes installation of a titanium armour bulkhead ahead of the cockpit and armour plates scabbed onto the sides of the cockpit; the overall effect is to improve crew protection by a factor of 1.36. Measures are also taken to shield vital fuel system components, increasing their protection by 42%; a new armoured lower fuselage skin prevents rapid total fuel loss if the aircraft is hit by ground fire, improving overall protection by 40%.

Another apparently minor but nevertheless useful modification is the addition of rear view mirrors on both sides of the cockpit canopy; these may give visual warning of a missile attack as the aircraft completes its bombing run. The Sukhoi Holding Co.'s upgrade includes the addition of more effective R-73 air-to-air missiles for self-defence replacing the earlier R-60M AAMs. At the ILA-2000 airshow held at Berlin-Schönefeld Sukhoi displayed a model of the Su-24M2 carrying the latest UAB-500 gliding guided bombs which can sail through the air for longer distances and hit the target with greater accuracy.

In a nutshell, despite its age the Su-24M still packs a punch and is able to accomplish a wide range of missions efficiently. A mid-life update would allow it to remain in service until sufficient numbers of next-generation combat aircraft are available.

Su-27SM, Su-27SKM and Su-27UBM Multi-Role Fighters

At the turn of the century, in parallel with the new-build Su-30MKI (for India), Su-30MKK (for China), Su-30MKM (for Malaysia) and Su-30MK2, the Sukhoi Holding Co. developed an upgrade package for the Russian Air Force's Su-27 single-seat fighters and

Originally modified as the Su-30KI demonstrator for an Indonesian order which failed to materialise, '305 Grey' (c/n 36911040102) later became the Su-27SKM demonstrator. The lightning bolt-shaped 'Danger, air intake' markings are noteworthy.

Air-to-surface guided weapons

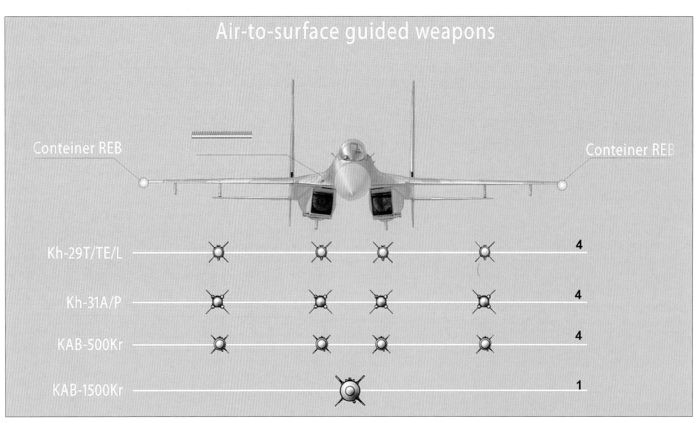

Conteiner REB

Conteiner REB

Kh-29T/TE/L	4
Kh-31A/P	4
KAB-500Kr	4
KAB-1500Kr	1

Air-to-surface unguided weapons

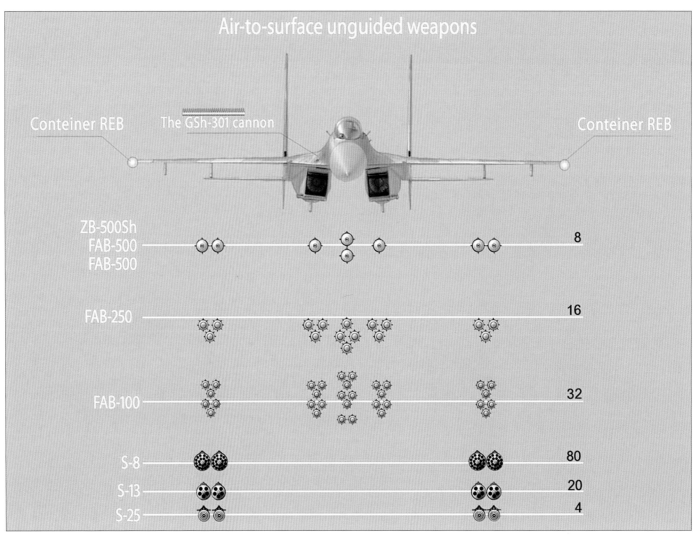

Conteiner REB

The GSh-301 cannon

Conteiner REB

ZB-500Sh FAB-500 FAB-500	8
FAB-250	16
FAB-100	32
S-8	80
S-13	20
S-25	4

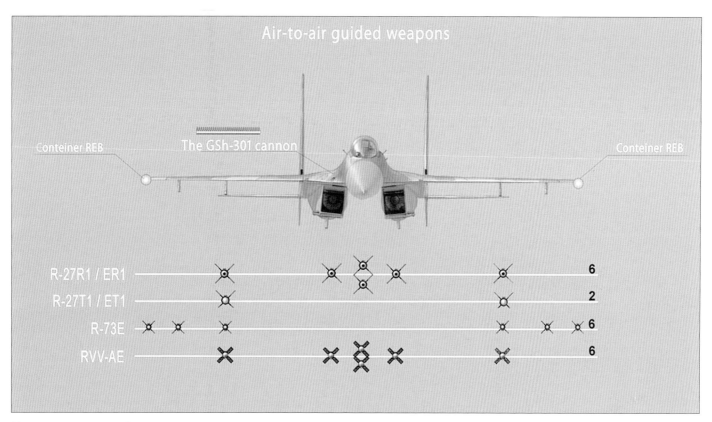

Air-to-air guided weapons

Conteiner REB   The GSh-301 cannon   Conteiner REB

R-27R1 / ER1	⊗	⊗ ⊗ ⊗	⊗	6
R-27T1 / ET1	⊗		⊗	2
R-73E	⊗ ⊗ ⊗		⊗ ⊗ ⊗	6
RVV-AE	⊗	⊗ ⊗ ⊗	⊗	6

Above and opposite page: These diagrams from a Sukhoi promotional CD-ROM (hence the unintelligible 'Conteiner REB' instead of 'ECM pod'!) illustrate the weapons options that can be carried by the Su-27SM, Su-27SKM and Su-27UBM. The Sorbtsiya ECM pods can be fitted instead of the usual wingtip missile rails; there are tandem pylons on the centreline. The triplets of bombs on the lower diagram on the opposite page are carried on MBD3-U6-68 multiple ejector racks.

Su-27UB combat trainers; the upgraded aircraft were designated Su-27SM and Su-27UBM respectively, the M standing for *modernizeerovannyy* (updated). Experts rate these aircraft as Generation 4+ fighters. The upgrade involves installation of modified engines and new avionics.

While the Su-27SM is intended for the Russian Air Force, an equivalent is offered to foreign customers as the Su-27SKM; traditionally for Sukhoi aircraft, the K stands for *kommehrcheskiy* ('commercial', that is, export version). According to Sukhoi spokesmen, the Su-27SKM is 50% more effective than the Su-27SK version supplied to China

(which also built it under licence) and Vietnam. Coded '305 Grey', the Su-27SKM prototype (c/n 36911040102) converted from the Su-27KI demonstrator made its debut at the MAKS-2003 airshow (19th-24th August 2003). It was also displayed at Airshow China 2004 (held at Zhuhai-Sanzao in November 2004), the 47th Paris Air Show in June 2005 and the MAKS-2005 airshow (16th-21st August 2005).

The export Su-27SKM differs from its Russian Air Force counterpart only in a few details – mostly in the identification friend-or-foe (IFF) system. The new guided weapons types are the same, regardless of what customer the aircraft is intended for.

Interestingly, the first upgraded *Flanker* delivered to the Russian Air Force was not a single-seater but a Su-27UBM combat trainer coded '20 Red' (formerly '62 Blue', c/n 96310420230). The official handover ceremony took place at Zhukovskiy on 6th March 2001. Subsequently the aircraft underwent comprehensive testing at the 929th GLITs, which lasted several years and included live weapons trials, and the pilots' appraisal was generally positive. On 14th-19th August 2001 Su-27UBM '20 Red' was in the static park of the MAKS-2001 airshow.

The Su-27SM prototype coded '56 Red' entered flight test shortly after the two-seater.

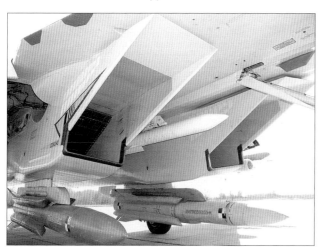

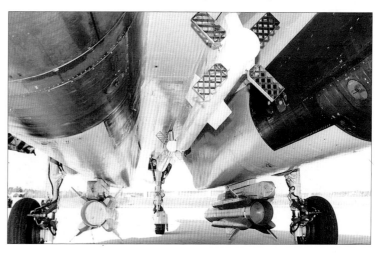

When displayed at the MAKS-2003 airshow the Su-27SKM carried dummy Kh-31A anti-shipping missiles under the engine nacelles and dummy R-77 (RVV-AE) AAMs on the centreline.

Above: Su-27SKM '305 Grey' with a full complement of dummy weapons. R-73 'dogfight missiles' are carried on the wingtip launch rails and the outboard wing pylons, with two R-77s on the centreline, two Kh-31s under the engine nacelles, a Kh-29T on the starboard inner wing pylon and an S-24 symmetrically to port.

Another view of the same aircraft at Zhukovskiy; this time Kh-29T air-to-surface missiles are carried on both inboard wing pylons. The retracted IFR probe is clearly visible; note the tactical code repeated on the inner faces of the fins and the 'Chinese-style' paint job encroaching on the radome (as on Chinese Su-27SK).

Above: The Su-27SKM makes a tight turn during a demonstration flight at one of the Moscow airshows. This view gives almost full details of the strange 'splatter' camouflage and shows the IRST unit offset to starboard to make room for the IFR probe. Note the code repeated on the trailing-edge flaps, US Navy style.

This fine picture of the Su-27SKM flying above thick overcast shows a configuration for attacking a surface target in the face of strong fighter opposition. Here, it has two dummy R-27ER long-range AAMs on the centreline and R-77s on the inboard wing pylons.

Above: The cockpit of the Su-27SKM (seen here in mock-up form) features two MFI-10 full-colour liquid-crystal multi-function displays, with an MFPI input/output device in between.

The trials of the Su-27SKM prototype and its demonstration flights abroad in the hope of attracting export orders proceeded in parallel.

The new technology incorporated into the Su-27SM/Su-27SKM increases the fighter's combat potential by 50% over the standard *Flanker-B* thanks first and foremost to the wider range of weaponry and the addition of strike capability. Combat efficiency is also helped by the new cockpit data presentation

and control systems and by the upgraded ECM/IRCM systems which increase the chances of survival in the face of heavy enemy anti-aircraft defences.

The performance of the navigation/attack suite is enhanced by the use of new operating algorithms and state-of-the-art electronic components. The modified N001 radar can perform ground mapping in actual beam mode, detecting ground targets with a high radar signature at up to 100 km (62 miles), large surface ships at up to 350 km (217 miles) and small ships at up to 120 km (74.5 miles). The Su-27SM/Su-27SKM is able to use TV-guided missiles (whose seeker heads receive initial target information from the air-craft's radar) and deliver bomb attacks in instrument meteorological conditions and at night. The weapons range includes Kh-29T/TE TV-guided missiles and Kh-29L laser-guided missiles, Kh-31A active radar homing anti-shipping missiles, Kh-31P anti-radiation missiles, KAB-500Kr and KAB-1500Kr 'smart bombs', R-77 (RVV-AE) active radar homing AAMs and more. All three upgraded versions of the *Flanker* – the Su-27SM/Su-27SKM and the Su-27UBM – feature an up-to-date ECM suite; additionally, the Su-27SM features a new ELINT/targeting system. The upgrade also includes a service life extension and measures aimed at improving reliability.

All three versions feature a new air-to-surface weapons control system (designated SUV-VEP1 in the version fitted to the export Su-27SKM). The cockpit features MFI-10 ten-inch liquid-crystal MFDs (***mno***gofoonktsio-

Su-27SKM '305 Grey' drops a KAB-500T TV-guided bomb.

nahl'nyy indikahtor) and an MFPI multi-function input/output device (**mno**gofoonktsio-**nahl**'nyy pool't-indi**kah**tor). Data exchange between the various avionics components takes places via high-speed multiplex data-buses. The new navigation suite incorporating a satellite navigation system receiver makes for much more accurate navigation and allows new data to be entered quickly from a memory card. The high-tech ELINT/targeting system with digital signal processing picks out the radar which is painting the aircraft, gives the pilot timely warning and quickly provides target information to the seeker head of the Kh-31P ARMs.

In air-to-air mode an increase in the Su-27SM/Su-27SKM's firepower is provided by modifications to the SUV-V weapons control system to permit carriage of R-77 (RVV-AE) AAMs. Higher survivability in the face of enemy air defences is ensured by an up-to-date ECM suite.

The Su-27SKM has a top speed of 1,400 km/h (869 mph) at sea level and 2,430 km/h (1,509 mph) at high altitude; the service ceiling is 18,000 m (59,055 ft) and the ferry range 3,680 km (2,285 miles). The maximum weapons load of 8,000 kg (17,640 lb) is carried on ten hardpoints. The operational G limit is 9 Gs.

Upon completion of the upgrade work, which was performed by the same Komsomol'sk-on-Amur Aircraft Production Association (KnAAPO) which had built the fighters, the first five Su-27SMs coded '02 Red', '03 Red', '04 Red' (c/n 36911018513), '06 Red' (c/n 36911019613) and '07 Red' were delivered to the Russian Air Force's 4th TsBP i PLS in Lipetsk in late December 2003. For starters the 'new' fighters were thoroughly mastered by the Centre's highly experienced pilots, including its Commander, Major General Aleksandr N. Kharchevskiy.

Top and above: The Su-27UBM prototype ('20 Red', c/n 96310420230) on a rain-soaked hardstand at Vladimirovka AB, Akhtoobinsk. Note the sheet metal jet blast deflectors.

The Su-27UBM in counter-air configuration during a test flight from Akhtoobinsk; the aircraft is armed with R-27T and R-73 AAMs.

Above: The Su-27UBM is outwardly indistinguishable from the standard Su-27UB, since the infra-red search & track (IRST) 'ball' ahead of the windshield is located centrally.

Here, a green-nosed Su-27UB coded '81 Red' formates with Su-27UBM '20 Red' over the estuary of the Volga River near Akhtoobinsk. The difference in camouflage patterns is noteworthy.

Above: '56 Red', the first in-service Su-27 to be upgraded to Su-27SM standard, is caught by the camera during final approach with only a pair of R-73s on the wingtip rails. Unlike the export Su-27SKM, the version for the home market lacks IFR capability – probably for cost reasons.

Another view of the same aircraft. It is rather unusual for Russian Air Force Su-27s to have the tactical code repeated in such large digits on the tails. Being the Su-27SM prototype, '56 Red' is used for test and development purposes.

Above and below: '07 Red', one of the first five Su-27s to be upgraded to Su-27SM standard, during an 'open house' at the 4th TsBP i PLS in Lipetsk which operates it. The aircraft is displayed with an impressive array of air-to-ground weapons, including FAB-100M-54 bombs, Kh-31 missiles and B-13L FFAR pods.

Another view of Su-27SM '07 Red' taxying at Lipetsk in unarmed configuration; note the three-tone camouflage.

The latter gained fame not only as the winner in a mock combat session with USAF pilots on their home ground during a goodwill visit to the USA but also, much later, as the only military pilot to take Russian President Vladimir V. Putin to Chechnya on an express inspection trip in the back seat of a Su-27UB.

The 4th TsBP i PLS evolved new operational procedures and combat tactics for the Su-27SM. Later, a number of ordinary service pilots took conversion training for the upgraded fighter, making it possible to start re-equipment of a first-line fighter unit – the 23rd IAP (*istrebitel'nyy aviapolk* – Fighter Regiment) stationed at Komsomol'sk-on-Amur/Dzemgi, which is both the KnAAPO factory airfield and a fighter base. The unit is part of the 11th Air Force/Air Defence Force Army pertaining to the Far Eastern Defence District. On 23rd December 2004 the 23rd IAP ceremonially took delivery of seven Su-27SMs, including '82 Red', '83 Red' and '84 Red'.

The delivery was made under a contract signed in 2004 by the Russian Air Force and KnAAPO. Under the terms of this contract 24 Su-27s home-based at Dzemgi were to be upgraded to Su-27SM standard in 2004-06; thus the 23rd IAP is to become the first Russian Air Force unit equipped entirely with upgraded aircraft. Speaking at the re-delivery ceremony, Russian Air Force Commander-in-Chief Army General (= four-star general) Vladimir Mikhaïlov said: 'The Su-27SM fully meets the requirements applied to present-

Above and below: '06 Red' (c/n 36911019613), another Su-27SM operated by the 4th TsBP i PLS, on the hardstand in Lipetsk with a solidly-built jet blast deflector in the background. Like '07 Red', it has differently coloured dielectric panels (the antenna fairing built into the starboard fin leading edge is green, not white).

Above: '06 Red' is readied for a sortie, with one of the Lipetsk centre's painted-up Su-27s *sans suffixe* ('61 Red') in the background; note also the finless R-60MU acquisition rounds beside the latter aircraft.

day military aircraft. The aircraft have a designated lifespan almost equal to that of new-build fighters but cost approximately seven times less. Yet, this upgraded Su-27SM can match the capabilities of the latest fighters and, if you'll excuse my saying so, excels the

Su-30MKK and the Su-30MKI taken collectively! That's because we have incorporated the best features of those aircraft into it. That's what I call an optimum upgrade!'

Since KnAAPO had insufficient export orders to keep the fighter production line fully

busy in 2005, the plant's General Director Viktor Merkoolov suggested completing the contract ahead of schedule (in 2005). This was a Mission Possible as far as the plant was concerned, but the defence budget for 2005 would not allow that.

Two close-ups of the cockpit of Su-27SM '06 Red'; the IRST 'ball' offset to starboard (despite the lack of an IFR probe) clearly identifies the upgraded aircraft. Note the cable connecting the canopy with the headrest of the K-36DM ejection seat; it triggers the seat's ejection gun when the canopy is jettisoned.

Su-27IB (Su-34, Su-32FN) Multi-Role Strike Aircraft

Quite recently the 929th GLITs added yet another aircraft to its impressive test fleet – the eighth example of the Su-27IB fighter-bomber (manufacturer's designation T-10V); this particular aircraft is known as the T10V-8 and appropriately coded '48 White outline'. Characterised by its sharp-chined 'platypus' nose and side-by-side seating for the crew of two, the first prototype of the Su-27's fighter-bomber derivative (hence the IB for *istrebitel'-bombardirovshchik*) made its first flight on 13th April 1990; the machine was designated T10V-1 and coded '42 Blue'. The second prototype (T10V-2 '43 Blue') followed on 18th December 1993; it differed from the first prototype mainly in having tandem-wheel main gear bogies instead of single large mainwheels and a longer tail 'stinger' which was to house a rear-warning radar. In this guise, according to the General Director and General Designer of what was then AVPK Sukhoi, the aircraft was soon redesignated Su-34 (obviously positioning it as a follow-on to the Su-24).

Shortly afterwards the Novosibirsk Aircraft Production Association (NAPO) named after Valeriy P. Chkalov, which had by then completed Su-24 production and was pretty much standing idle, began manufacturing a pre-series batch. This included the T10V-4 ('44 White outline', c/n 4160662700573), the T10V-5 ('45 White outline'), the T10V-6 ('46 White outline') and the T10V-7 ('47 White outline'). At this stage the aircraft received the alternative designation Su-32FN under which it was to be offered for export; no official explanation of the FN suffix has ever been given, although some sources allege it stands for 'fighter, naval'.

Above: Su-27SM '02 Red' parked at Lipetsk with a protective cover over the cockpit canopy.

Above: Yet another Su-27SM, '03 Red', takes off from Komsomol'sk-on-AMur/Dzemgi, bound for Lipetsk.

Su-27SM '04 Red' (c/n 36911018513) in the static park of the MAKS-2005 airshow. Note the dummy Kh-31 missile under the port wing, the Sapsan target designator pod under the port engine nacelle and the KAB-500Kr-U fixed 'smart bomb' acquisition round under the starboard engine nacelle.

Opposite page, above and below: Two more views of Su-27SM '04 Red' at the MAKS-2005. The upper picture creates the impression that the Sapsan pod is attached upside down. In fact, however, the front end of the pod incorporating the optical window rotates through 360° for engaging targets to the left or right of the aircraft's flight path and is rotated upside down for take-off and landing to protect the window from damage by debris kicked up by the nosewheel. The lower picture shows the front end of the pod rotated into operational position.

Right and below: The same aircraft at a different air event; the relative position of the Sapsan pod and the KAB-500Kr-U acquisition round is reversed. Note the adapters needed for carrying the two pods and the revolving 'head' of the Sapsan pod.

Bottom: Three views of the ceremony at KnAAPO on 23rd December 2004 when the 23rd IAP took delivery of its Su-27SMs. Note the almost-complete Beriyev Be-103 amphibian in the right-hand picture.

Su-27SM '06 Red' in action: taking off on a sortie (top) and immediately after coming home (centre and above). Unless advanced weapons are hooked up to give the upgrade away, the Su-27SM looks just like any ordinary *Flanker-B*.

Top: Pictured here at Komsomol'sk-on-Amur/Dzemgi, this Su-27SM, '80 Red', was later transferred to Lipetsk for some reason.
Centre and above: Operational Su-27SMs at Komsomol'sk-on-Amur/Dzemgi.

Above: A pilot climbs into the cockpit of a Su-27SM. Note the fitting on his ZSh-7 flying helmet which may be an attachment for a helmet-mounted sight.

Above: A pre-production Su-34 nearing completion at the Novosibirsk Aircraft Production Association. Note the chrome yellow primer finish.

Whatever the case, the Russian military are adamant that the T-10V's service designation shall be Su-27IB, not Su-34; their argument is 'the aircraft was designed to meet our specifications and paid for with our money'. There may be one more reason for this obstinacy – the wish to underscore the aircraft's 'family ties' with the basic Su-27, the Soviet/Russian Air Force's principal fighter type at the end of the 20th century; this may make it easier to secure state funding for the advanced and valuable new aircraft. Here the Su-27IB harks back to its precursor, the Su-24, which also started life 'in disguise' for much the same reason. At the preliminary design stage the future *Fencer* was known at the Sukhoi OKB as the T-58M; this was a ploy meant to pass the bomber off as 'just another version' of the totally unrelated T-58 interceptor – the Su-15 *Flagon*. This was because during the Khrushchov era, given Nikita S. Khrushchov's famous predilection towards missile systems, money for 'clean sheet of paper' combat aircraft projects was all but impossible to obtain, and the government officials would never know the difference anyway. Later, when the funding had been secured, the OKB dropped the masquerade and the bomber received the new in-house designation T-6. Nevertheless, the management of AVPK Sukhoi was very active promoting the Su-34 and (especially) Su-32FN designations which were picked up with relish and perpetuated by the Russian and foreign media.

The Su-27IB's development and service introduction has been one of the Russian Air Force's top-priority programmes for several years now.

Now, a few details about the aircraft itself. The Su-27IB has a crew of two (a pilot and a navigator/WSO). It is powered by two Lyul'ka AL-31F afterburning turbofans rated at 12,500 kgp (27,560 lbst) in full afterburner.

'43 Blue', the second prototype Su-27IB/Su-34 (the T10V-2), taxies at Zhukovskiy. Note the extended and recontoured (more pointed) tail 'stinger' which houses additional equipment for a special test programme.

Two views of the T10V-2 during trials. The aircraft carries three 1,500-kg (3,306-lb) KAB-1500L laser-guided bombs on the forward centreline and inboard wing stations, FAB-250M-54 'dumb bombs' on MBD3-U6-68 MERs on the engine nacelle and outboard wing hardpoints, and R-60Ms for self-defence.

Left: The flightdeck of one of the Su-27IB (Su-34) development aircraft. The instrumentation is largely electromechanical, with three MFDs and a multi-function input/output panel in the centre of the instrument panel. Note the red emergency braking handle underneath the I/O panel and the twin ejection handles of the K-36DM seats.

Below left: The flightdeck of a later Su-34 with an updated mission avionics suite. Note the additional MFD (equipped with a rubber sunblind) and I/O panel supplanting most of the conventional instruments at the WSO's workstation. This is not the definitive version yet!

Right: '45 White outline' (the T10V-5), the third Su-27IB (Su-34) to fly, at an 'open house' in Akhtoobinsk; the radome has been removed, exposing the antenna of the phased-array radar. The latter turned out to be a lemon and was later replaced by a new radar from a different manufacturer.

Below: The Su-27IB's flightdeck is accessed via the nosewheel well; the doorway is seen from the ground (below) and from the flightdeck (below right). Note the access ladder and the avionics bay aft of the flightdeck in the right-hand picture.

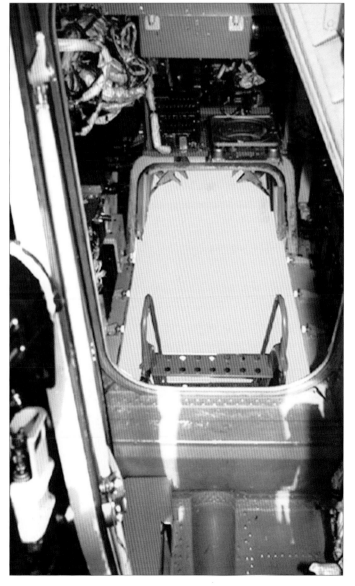

Above: Two views of the flightdeck section of the T10V-8 ('48 White outline'), the newest Su-27IB (Su-34) as of this writing. The roof sections above the seats are jettisoned before ejection; the olive drab anti-glare panel extends to the windshield frame.

Above: The GSh-301 cannon is buried in the starboard leading-edge root extension, just like on all other Su-27 variants. The small size of the blast panel is noteworthy.

The maximum take-off weight approaches 45 tons (99,200 lb), including up to 8,000 kg (17,640 lb) of ordnance. The top speed is approximately 1,900 km/h (1,180 mph) or Mach 1.8 at high altitude and 1,400 km/h (869 mph) at sea level. Effective range on internal fuel at high altitude is some 4,000 km (2,484 miles), increasing to some 7,000 km (4,347 miles) with one in-flight refuelling, and ferry range is some 4,500 km (2,795 miles). With

in-flight refuelling the Su-27IB can patrol and wage combat for up to 16 hours; this naturally required the designers to provide maximum comfort for the crew so as to reduce fatigue. The cockpit (or rather flightdeck) is a welded capsule made of titanium armour; it is accessible from below (via the nosewheel well) and is spacious enough to stand tall in. The ejection seats have a built-in massage feature (!) and are installed with an aisle in between, allowing the crewmembers to walk around (one at a time) and stretch their legs if the tactical situation allows. A galley and a toilet are located in a compartment aft of the seats.

The Su-27IB (Su-34) can use an extraordinarily wide range of weapons, including precision-guided munitions (PGMs). The ability to use virtually the entire range of air-to-air missiles makes it a true multi-role combat aircraft. The machine is chock-full of avionics catering for navigation/ground mapping, target detection, weapons guidance, ELINT, ECM and information warfare (providing the enemy with false target parameters). The aircraft features an SAU-10V automatic flight control system developed by MNPK Avionika ('Avionics' Moscow Scientific & Production Complex); it ensures control of the aircraft in

Two views of FAB-250M-54 bombs on MBD3-U6-68 multiple ejector racks and a KAB-1500L guided bomb on the hardpoints of a Su-27IB (Su-34). Only five out of a possible six bombs are carried on each MER for payload limit reasons.

Top and above: The T10V-7 ('47 White outline') parked in front of a modular jet blast deflector at Vladimirovka AB, Akhtoobinsk. It is loaded with an unusual mix of ordnance comprising a KAB-1500L 'smart bomb', FAB-250M-54 'dumb bombs', Kh-31 ASMs, R-27Rs, R-60Ms and R-77 acquisition rounds.

Left: Su-34 '45 White outline' in an as-yet infrequently seen formation with a sister ship (unfortunately not identifiable) over the estuary of the Volga River. The differently coloured radomes are noteworthy; note also the Le Bourget exhibit code 347.

Below left: Another view of '45 White outline' as it maintains close line-astern formation with the camera ship. The black stripes on the radome are photo calibration markings.

Right: The T10V-4 ('44 White outline', Le Bourget exhibit code 343) fires a ripple of S-13 unguided rockets from four B-13L pods. The white stuff above the jet is not cloud or contrails from another aircraft but smoke from already launched rockets.

Below and bottom: The same aircraft unleashes a salvo of four S-25-OFM heavy unguided rockets whose bulged warheads are larger in diameter than the disposable launch tubes. The rockets produce terrific flames as they go!

Above: '48 White outline' is the first Su-27IB (Su-34) to actually have the Sorbtsiya wingtip ECM pods featured on several display models. All Su-27IBs/Su-34s except the first two prototypes have this garish 'greenbottle fly' camouflage but the pattern differs from aircraft to aircraft.

automatic (autopilot) and flight director mode. The AFCS has built-in test equipment (BITE) which constantly monitors its own hardware and that of associated systems, automatically disabling a flight mode if the equipment supporting it goes unserviceable and running an automated pre-flight check.

The automated weapons control system and armament enable the Su-27IB to launch pre-emptive strikes against any targets, including small ones. The aircraft can engage and destroy the latest air superiority fighters, as well as ECM aircraft, airborne early warning and control (AWACS) aircraft and airborne command posts (ABCPs). In strike mode the Su-27IB can perform suppression of enemy air defences (SEAD) and attack maritime and ground targets while staying out of range of the enemy's anti-aircraft weapons. The missile and bomb armament carried on the aircraft's 12 hardpoints includes up to six Kh-31P anti-radiation missiles and/or Kh-31A anti-shipping missiles; the latter have warheads powerful enough to sink or cripple any surface ship, even an aircraft carrier. A maritime version equipped with a suitable avionics suite, such as the latest *Morskoy Zmey* (Sea Serpent) suite created by the Leninets Holding Co. in St. Petersburg, can fill the anti-submarine warfare (ASW) role in the shallow coastal waters. The Morskoy Zmey can detect surface ships at a maximum range of 320 km (198 miles); in ASW/submarine search mode performs up to 3.3 billion operations per second. The suite has an automatic target identification/threat assessment/target tracking

Su-34 '48 White outline' displays its upper surfaces in a tight turn to port.

mode, controlling up to 32 surface and submerged targets at a time.

The first two prototypes (the T10V-1 and T10V-2) were built by the Sukhoi OKB's prototype construction shop in Moscow. Subsequent prototypes and pre-production machines were manufactured by NAPO in Novosibirsk; the six aircraft built there in 1993-2003 are currently at the concluding stage of the state acceptance trials. As of now the Russian Air Force has a whole list of major complaints concerning the avionics suite, and the problems have to be addressed before the Su-27IB is officially included in the Russian Air Force inventory in 2006. Hence the sixth Novosibirsk-built example (the T10V-8) was manufactured in fully-equipped representative production configuration. Russian Air Force C-in-C Vladimir Mikhaïlov said in a press interview that 'the configuration of this aircraft is the one which will remain in Air Force service for a long time'. He went on to say that seven examples have been manufactured (Mikhaïlov was referring to the flight test articles, as the T10V-3 was apparently a static test airframe – Author), the test programme has been completed and the aircraft has been recommended for Air Force service. 'I have suspended the [tests of the] No.8 aircraft so that the avionics can be replaced with better ones', said Mikhaïlov, pointing out that the Su-27IB's development has been pro-

Above: An early artist's impression of the 'big head' Su-27KUB naval trainer. Note the four weapons hardpoints on each wing giving a total of 12.

tracted and the avionics have become obsolete before the aircraft had a chance to enter service. According to Mikhaïlov, the avionics of the T10V-8 have considerable commonality with those fitted to the upgraded Su-27SM fighter. The C-in-C says the Su-27IB's production entry depends entirely on whether the Russian MoD can afford it. 'Just give us the money, and the quantity [of Su-27IBs] will grow steadily', said the general, stressing that the Air Force plans to keep the Su-27IB (Su-34) for quite a time. According to Russian press reports, NAPO plans to deliver five more examples in 2006-07.

Of course, the Su-27IB costs a bundle; but then, the Russian Air Force and the Russ-

ian Naval Air Arm do not have to order large numbers of Su-27IBs by all means, as had been the case with the Su-24. The new multi-role combat aircraft can act as a mini-ABCP controlling the concerted actions of other tactical aircraft.

Su-27KUB Shipboard Multi-Role Aircraft

Inevitably dubbed *Koob* (Cube), the Su-27KUB (*korabel'nyy oochebno-boyevoy* [*samolyot*] – shipboard combat-capable trainer) represents a major modification of the production Su-33 (Su-27K) fighter now equipping the carrier wing of Russia's sole conventional take-off and landing (CTOL) aircraft

During the initial flight test phase the Su-27KUB prototype was flown in this 'patchwork' finish. The amount of primer on the new structural components emphasises how little is left of the original Su-27K (the fifth prototype, T10K-5, '59 Blue') airframe from which it was converted.

Above: An interesting formation of the *Flanker*'s single-seat and two-seat naval versions as '72 Red', an operational Su-33 of the 279th Shipboard Fighter Regiment stationed aboard the RNS *Admiral Kuznetsov*, leads the Su-27KUB prototype at the MAKS-2001 airshow in Zhukovskiy.

carrier RNS *Admiral Kuznetsov*). When ordering its development the Russian MoD fully realised that due to budgetary constraints the Navy cannot afford to operate a wide range of types and commonality is the key to success.

The two-seat Su-27KUB is to become a versatile and potent weapon which will not only provide protection for the aircraft carrier but also fulfil a broad spectrum of naval aviation tasks. The programme had reached an advanced stage by the end of 2005, and the Russian Naval Air Arm counts on the deliveries to begin in a few years.

On 6th October 1999 the unpainted and uncoded Su-27KUB prototype (later coded '21 Blue', c/n 49051002502) successfully made its first carrier landing on the RNS *Admiral Kuznetsov* – less than six months after the maiden flight from Zhukovskiy. The subsequent tests were accompanied by a fair share of trouble and one mission nearly proved fatal. On 16th June 2000 the Su-27KUB suffered structural failure after encountering a hitherto unknown and dangerous flight mode (the test mission, which was flown from Zhukovskiy, involved low-level flight at the aircraft's never-exceed speed). The crew's experience and excellent airmanship saved the day; Sukhoi OKB test pilots Viktor G. Pugachov (holder of the Merited Test Pilot

Another aspect of the Su-27KUB at the MAKS-2001 airshow. As compared to the standard Su-27K (Su-33), the two-seater has greater wing and tailplane area, taller vertical tails and larger canard foreplanes with raked tips. Note that originally the canards had a straight leading edge.

and Hero of the Soviet Union titles) and Roman P. Taskayev managed to bring the crippled aircraft safely home.

An urgent redesign was begun and changes were made to the structure of the Su-27KUB as the aircraft was undergoing repairs. On 19th December 2000 Viktor G. Pugachov and Sergey Bogdan performed the first post-repair checkout flight; just two days later the aircraft was flown to Novofyodorovka AB in the town of Saki on the Crimea Peninsula, the Ukraine, for further tests. (This base, which hosts the famous *Nitka* (Thread) 'unsinkable carrier' training facility, is on long-tem lease to Russia.) By the end of the year the three Sukhoi test pilots flying the Su-27KUB (Pugachov, Bogdan and Taskayev) had been joined by their colleagues from the Russian Air Force's 929th GLITs – Col. A. M. Rayevskiy, Col. N. F. Diorditsa and Col. V. S. Petroosha.

The first tests of any importance on the Su-27KUB in which 929th GLITs personnel participated took place at the Nitka installation in December 2000/January 2001. The programme involved checking the aircraft's field performance during ski-jump take-offs and arrested landings at various weights up to the maximum take-off and landing weights. The Air Force test pilots were in for a pleasant surprise: the aircraft performed better than they had hoped. Still, production and service were still far away and a lot more test work was needed before they could materialise.

Tests on the 'unsinkable carrier' resumed in the spring of 2002. Apart from the usual ski-jump take-offs and arrested landings, they included tests of the Zhuk-MS (Beetle-MS) slotted-array fire control radar; among other things, the radar's ground mapping mode was verified. After that, the Su-27KUB returned to Moscow for more modifications. Thus, in 2003 the new *Sokol* (Falcon) radar was installed; this radar is a version of the Zhuk-MS with a new phased antenna array, hence the alternative designation Zhuk-MSF (F = *fazeerovannaya antennaya reshotka* – phased array). The new radar is expected to give the 'Cube' a major boost in combat potential.

Top: The cockpit section of the Su-27KUB bears a strong similarity to that of the Su-27IB (Su-34) but is nevertheless very different, lacking the large 'hump' aft of it and featuring an ogival radome and IRST 'ball'. Note the very large gun blast plate.

Centre: This head-on view shows the revised canards with a cranked leading edge; Note the test equipment sensors in a yellow 'chewing gum' compound.

Right: In 2005 the Su-27KUB was retrofitted with thrust-vectoring engines whose nozzles are seen here at maximum downward deflection.

Top and centre: Front views with the two-section flaps partially and fully deployed, the ailerons drooped and (centre) the airbrake deployed.
Above: This rear view shows how the wide forward fuselage tapers off into the characteristic spine or 'stinger' between the engine nozzles.

These three views of the Su-27KUB taxying at Novofyodorovka AB, Saki, show well the upper fuselage contour. The additional port side landing lights visible on the photo on page 42 have been deleted. Note that the star insignia lack the customary white surround, which gives them a measure of 'low-observability'.

Opposite page: Two more views of the Su-27KUB taxying at Saki. Note that test equipment sensors embedded in that yellow compound are found all over the airframe. The IFR probe and the Russian Navy flag are clearly visible.

Right: Seen from this angle, the Su-27KUB pops up like a jack-in-the-box as it leaves the T-2 ski jump of the Nitka 'unsinkable carrier' at Novofyodorovka AB. The installation replicates the ski jump of the real carrier.

Below: The Su-27KUB makes a low-speed pass, showing the flap design and the ventral blow-in 'gills'. No weapons pylons, apart from the wingtip missile rails, are fitted. Note the retracted arrester hook and the setting of the canards. The wing folding joints are located farther outboard than on the single-seat Su-33.

Bottom: The Su-27KUB makes a 'carrier approach' with the arrester hook deployed, ready to catch the wire of the arrester system at Novofyodorovka AB.

Another important change was the fitment of experimental AL-31F Srs 3 engines with thrust-vectoring nozzles; AL-31FP engines with similar nozzles giving pitch-only thrust vectoring control (TVC) power the Indian Air Force's Su-30MKI. This modification gives a major improvement in agility and field performance. It was in this guise (with thrust-vectoring engines and the new radar) that the Su-27KUB underwent renewed carrier compatibility trials in the High North in November 2004; the aircraft was flown by Sukhoi and 929th GLITs pilots. In August 2005 the Su-27KUB was in the static park of the MAKS-2005 airshow – although most of the visitors overlooked the thrust-vectoring engines.

The top command of the Russian Naval Air Arm intends to adopt the Su-27KUB as the future standard aircraft that will replace several current types at once – both shipboard and shore-based. If these plans materialise (as usual, this depends largely on the funding), the 'Cube' will supersede the single-seat Su-33 aboard the RNS *Admiral Kuznetsov* and supplant the Su-24M, and possibly even the Tupolev Tu-22M3 heavy bomber, in the Russian Navy's attack and bomber regiments. The Su-27KUB's service entry will facilitate the training of shipboard fighter pilots considerably. Pilots note the equally good (and, importantly, almost identical) field of view from the left-hand and right-hand seats, which is crucial while practising carrier landings. As regards agility and handling, the Su-27KUB is much closer to the Su-33 than the subsonic Su-25UTG trainer currently used for conversion/proficiency training.

Opposite page: The Su-25SM prototype, '19 Red' (c/n 25508110219), undergoing conversion at the Russian Air Force's Aircraft Repair Plant (ARZ) No.121 at Kubinka AB in company with a MiG-29 and a Su-27. Note the extended boarding ladder/steps.

Right: The engineering personnel of ARZ No.121 and Sukhoi test pilot Roman Kondrat'yev pose beside the upgraded aircraft sporting 'Su-25SM' nose titles and the badge of the repair plant ahead of the windshield. The vehicle is a 7,500-litre (1,650 Imp gal) TZA-7.5-500A fuel bowser based on the MAZ-5335 lorry. Note the An-12BPs of the resident transport regiment in the background beyond the runway.

Below: Fitted with four drop tanks, Su-25SM '19 Red' is ready for a ferry flight.

Bottom: Another view of the Su-25SM prototype on the taxiway of ARZ No.121 on the south side of Kubinka AB, with a pool of MiG-29s awaiting overhaul in the background.

Above: The Su-25SM displays its underside as it makes a farewell pass over Kubinka.

The same aircraft undergoing trials at the 929th State Flight Test Centre at Vladimirovka AB, Akhtoobinsk. The aircraft carries UB-32M and B-13L rocket pods, MERs loaded with bombs, and R-60MU acquisition rounds.

Top and above: '33 Red', the second Su-25SM, stripped down for the upgrade.

Su-25SM Upgraded Attack Aircraft

It is a well-known fact that Soviet Air Force units flying Su-25 attack aircraft were originally regarded as no more than a 'supplement' to the mighty fist of fighter-bomber regiments operating the Su-17 and MiG-27. In a war scenario, the Su-25s were to perform a very limited range of missions. In the 1990s, however, the Russian Air Force's fighter-bomber arm vanished altogether (as a result of the decision to withdraw single-engined types), leaving the Su-25 as the sole Russian light attack aircraft. This brought about the need to expand the *Frogfoot*'s range of applications, turning the Su-25 into a multi-role weapons system capable of filling the fighter-bomber and, to a certain degree, even the tactical bomber role. The 'classic' attack aircraft could make do with a fairly simple navigation/attack suite enabling attacks in a shallow dive – well, mostly. Now the Russian Air Force's new needs (and the resulting upgrade) required the installation of more complex and capable navigation and targeting equipment enabling accurate location of the target which would then be attacked with bombs in level flight.

Despite wearing 'Su-25SM' nose titles and the badge of ARZ No.121, '33 Red' displayed at the MAKS-2001 airshow was actually still an ordinary Su-25 *sans suffixe* then. It would be a few more years before this particular aircraft would become what it was advertised to be.

Another reason that prompted the upgrade was that the Su-25's analogue avionics, dating back to the late 1960s, were hopelessly outdated and were running out of service life. The radically changed situation on the battlefield which attack aircraft would have to face was a further factor. Initially, apart from enemy fighters, it was mobile anti-aircraft artillery (AAA) and small-arms fire that was regarded as the main threat, and the Su-25's survivability features were designed accordingly. Nowadays an aircraft operating over the forward edge of the battle area or behind enemy lines has to deal with a growing range of ever more potent army air defence assets, from shoulder-launched surface-to-air missiles to high-mobility SAM, combined SAM/AAA or AAA systems with radar, TV, infrared or laser guidance.

Therefore, the upgrade centres on increasing the Su-25's killing power by radically improving the delivery accuracy of free-fall bombs and unguided rockets, the cheapest and most widespread strike weapons, and by reducing the error margin to 5-10 m (16-33 ft). Such a fairly low-cost upgrade would allow the mission to be accomplished by a much smaller number of aircraft, thereby reducing own losses.

Here it should be noted that the single-seat Su-25 *sans suffixe* had been produced in Tbilisi and that production had come to a standstill after Georgia gained independence when the Soviet Union broke up. Hence in the 1990s the Ulan-Ude Aircraft Production Association (U-UAPO), which until then had built the Su-25UB combat-capable trainer, started gearing up to produce the most advanced version of the *Frogfoot* – the tank-busting Su-25T. Based on the 'hunchback' airframe of the trainer, this single-seater was equipped with the new Shkval (Gale) and armed with Vikhr' (Whirlwind) advanced beam-riding high-velocity anti-tank guided missiles. The SUV-25T *Voskhod* (Sunrise) weapons control system (*sistema oopravleniya vo'oroozheniyem* – WCS), aka *izdeliye* (product) 8PM, provided round-the-clock navigation and targeting capability, and the target detection/engagement process was highly automated. Later, the Su-25T was to be superseded on the production line by the even more advanced Su-25TM (Su-39) featuring the new and smarter SUO-39 digital WCS (*sistema oopravleniya oroozhiyem* – WCS). This version carried a *Kinzhal* (Dagger) ultra-high-resolution radar or a Kop'yo miniature pulse-Doppler radar in a large ventral pod. The Kinzhal radar developed by the St. Petersburg-based NPO Leninets (Leninist, now the Leninets Holding Company; NPO = *naoochno-proizvodstvennoye obyedineniye* – Scientific & Production Association) can detect objects several dozen centimetres

long. The *Kop'yo-25* (Spear-25) radar developed by the Fazotron-NIIR corporation is a version of the radar fitted to the upgraded MiG-21-93 fighter; it turned the Su-25TM into a true multi-role combat aircraft capable of beyond visual range (BVR) aerial combat, using R-77 (RVV-AE) medium-range AAMs.

The Soviet Air Force did take delivery of a handful of production Su-25TMs prior to the demise of the Soviet Union; however, funding of the Su-25TM programme was greatly reduced with the onset of President Mikhail S. Gorbachov's *perestroika* (and the attendant arms reduction efforts) and vanished altogether in post-Soviet days. Given the lack of further new-build examples, ideas were voiced about converting Su-25UBs to Su-25TM standard at the Russian Air Force's ARZ No.121 (*aviaremontnyy zavod* – Aircraft Overhaul Plant) at Kubinka AB west of Moscow. However, for various reasons (mostly due to lack of funding) the 'tank killer' versions never entered Russian Air Force service. Also, the Air Force was not too happy with the examples it already had: these were tested by the Air Force Research Institute (GNIKI VVS) in Akhtoobinsk which later transferred several Su-25Ts to the 4th TsBP i PLS for evaluation. The Su-25T even saw action in the Chechen Wars but the pilots did not rate it highly – mainly because of the troublesome new mission avionics.

Above: The forward fuselage of Su-25SM c/n 25508110139; the sticker on the nose identifies it as the T8SM-5, that is, the fifth upgraded aircraft.

Considering all of the above, the Sukhoi Holding Co. decided to offer several upgrade packages for the operational Su-25s, which suited the Russian Air Force just fine. The option selected eventually was fairly radical, envisaging an almost complete replacement of the avionics; only the Klyon-PS (Maple-PS) laser ranger/marked target seeker remained of the original avionics, and even that was due for replacement with a more modern unit latter on. Nevertheless, the upgrade was affordable.

Designated Su-25SM and known in-house as the T-8SM, the upgraded aircraft looks just like any Su-25 but the innards are completely different. Its custom-made Bars (Leopard) navigation/attack suite includes a TsVM-90 digital processor developed by the

Another view of the same aircraft. Bearing no tactical code at the moment of the upgrade, this aircraft used to be coded '12 Red' when stationed in East Germany; it now belongs to an attack regiment based in Budyonnovsk, Stavropol' Region, not far from the Chechen Theatre of Operations.

St. Petersburg-based Elektroavtomatika OKB. The instrument panel features a colour MFD displaying flight, navigation and tactical information. The latter is presented as a digital map showing the position of the frontline, known enemy air defence assets and the areas they cover and so on.

The Su-25SM features a combined inertial/satellite navigation suite giving an error margin of 200 m (660 ft) in autonomous mode of 50 m (164 ft) with satellite correction. Bombing accuracy in level flight at 200-300 m (660-990 ft) using 'dumb bombs' is 10-15 m (33-49 ft), which matches the performance of the US JDAM (Joint Direct Attack Munition) 'smart bomb'.

One of the main concepts followed by the authors of the Su-25SM's avionics suite is that the pilot's actions in the course of the attack should be simplified as much as possible, allowing him to concentrate on the flying. The targeting procedures are automated insofar as possible, requiring a minimum of pilot input. This also results in a simple and uncluttered cockpit which makes the aircraft easier to fly and fight in.

The ASP-17BTs-8 gunsight is replaced by a wide-angle HUD which is the pilot's primary instrument when attacking a ground target. The HUD features an ultra-bright cathode-ray tube making the information clearly readable even in strong sunlight; it displays all necessary piloting and target information, making sure that the pilot is not distracted in the course of the attack.

The new avionics have given a substantial weight saving of around 300 kg (660 lb). As a result, some avionics items have been relocated from the rear fuselage, which is most likely to take punishment in a missile attack, to a safer place in the fuselage nose. Unlike the standard aircraft, which has only R-60 or R-60M AAMs for self-defence, the Su-25SM can carry more effective R-73 'dogfight AAMs'; advanced ASMs are to be integrated later on.

As on the earlier Su-25T, the engines feature surge protection to stop them from flaming out after ingesting rocket/missile blast gases and smoke. This expands the Su-25SM's combat envelope. Survivability enhancement measures (some of which were incorporated on late-production Su-25s *sans suffixe*) include a duplex fire suppression system, fireproof push-pull rods in the control system and additional armour plate.

The combined effect of these modifications turns the Su-25SM into a virtually new aircraft whose combat efficiency is increased by 50-100%. The resulting aircraft meets the Russian Air Force's current requirements in full.

The prototype coded '19 Red' (c/n 25508110219) was upgraded by ARZ No.121. The aircraft made its public debut at the MAKS-2003 airshow; it was also displayed at the Hydro Aviation Show '04 in Ghelendjik and at the MAKS-2005. Currently several more Su-25s are being upgraded at Kubinka AB, but the prospects of the Su-25SM's service entry remain unclear.

The cockpit of the T8SM-5 (Su-25SM c/n 25508110139), showing the MFD and the new head-up display.

Chapter 2

Modernising the MiG-29

The Mikoyan MiG-29, which has earned universal recognition as one of the world's best light fighters, became a key component of the Russian Air Force's fighter fleet in the late 20th century. Its development continued in the 21st century, and this chapter deals with the fighter's latest versions.

MiG-29SMT (MiG-29SMT2) Single-Seat Multi-Role Fighter (*izdeliye* 9.18)

Currently the MiG Russian Aircraft Corp. (RSK MiG) is pursuing a number of MiG-29 upgrade programmes to meet orders from the Russian Ministry of Defence and several foreign customers. These include the MiG-29SMT multi-role fighter. The designation may sound a bit misleading, as several upgraded MiG-29s had been tested in the 1990s under the MiG-29SMT designation. These aircraft were known in-house as *izdeliye* 9.17 and, interestingly, the avionics fit had changed with each successive change of the company leader.

The original version of *izdeliye* 9.17 had been outfitted by the Roosskaya Avionika (Russian Avionics) company whose boss Mikhail Korzhooyev also headed ANPK MiG at the time. When Nikolay F. Nikitin took over as General Director of ANPK MiG, the MiG-29SMT received a new avionics suite based on that of the MiG-29M (*izdeliye* 9.15) fighter prototypes.

In contrast, the aircraft described here could be called the 'second-generation' MiG-29SMT (hence it is sometimes referred to as the MiG-29SMT2). Its flight and mission avionics (WCS) have substantial commonality with the latest versions of the MiG-29 now under development – the revamped MiG-29K/MiG-29KUB and the 're-upgraded' MiG-29M/MiG-29M2 which are described separately.

In accordance with the design ideology of the 'new' MiG-29SMT (aka *izdeliye* 9.18) the fighter's technical outlook is determined by the customer in accordance with his require-

ments – and his wallet. In other words, the *izdeliye* 9.18 has no 'standard' version and is tailored to the needs of each specific customer by combining three basic upgrade packages as required.

The first basic package comprises an upgrade of the WCS which turns the air superiority fighter into a multi-role combat aircraft. The MiG-29SMT (*izdeliye* 9.18) features a Zhuk-ME radar developed by Fazotron-NIIR specially for new versions of the *Fulcrum*. This is a pulse-Doppler radar with a mechanically scanned slotted array intended for medium and heavy fighters; the Zhuk-ME has passed a complete cycle of ground and flight tests (the latter were performed on modified MiG-29s), meeting its performance target in full. The radar can operate in ground-attack, mapping, weather (storm warning) and terrain following modes. As compared to the N019 fitted to production *Fulcrums*, the Zhuk-ME offers 50% greater aerial target

Aptly coded '917 Blue', the first prototype MiG-29SMT (*izdeliye* 9.17; c/n 2960535400, f/n 4710) is shown here in its 2005 guise – that is, in the garish camouflage applied for the MAKS-2005 airshow. The extraordinarily fat spine holding extra fuel and the strap-on IFR probe are visible.

Above and below: Head-on views of MiG-29SMT '917 Blue' armed with four Kh-29T air-to-surface missiles and and R-77 (RVV-AE) AAMs.

detection range and the ability to attack two priority threats at a time and introduces the abovementioned air-to-ground modes with a resolution of 5x5 m (16.5x16.5 ft); Fazotron-NIIR is working on enhancing the resolution to 3x3 m (10x10 ft). Of the many radars created by the corporation in recent years the Zhuk-ME turned out to be the best option for the MiG-29's new versions, beating even the seemingly more advanced Zhuk-MFE electronically-scanned phased-array radar. The Zhuk-ME is produced in quantity at Fazotron-NIIR's own manufacturing facilities.

Apart from its early aircraft radars, Fazotron-NIIR is well known for the Kop'yo radar intended for upgrading the MiG-21*bis* fighter. A MiG-21*bis* retrofitted with the Kop'yo radar can wage aerial combat against even the latest fighters at long, medium and short

Above: MiG-29SMT '918 White' (c/n 2960536050, f/n 4815) with an impressive array of weapons at the MAKS-2003 airshow. The aircraft is painted in a desert camouflage.

Centre and above: '918 White' retains the standard *Fulcrum-A* fuselage contour. The 'SMT' titles are in Cyrillic characters to port and in Roman characters to starboard. The aircraft carries the flags of the nations operating the MiG-29, including Yemen, hence *izdeliye* 9.18 has been called 'the Yemeni version'.

range. The Zhuk-ME was developed by the same design team, using the same components; however, the corporation took into account the experience with the Kop'yo accumulated by the Indian Air Force and is working on increasing the Zhuk-ME's reliability to several times that of the older model.

The MiG-29SMT's upgraded WCS makes the fighter compatible with a much wider range of air-to-air and guided/unguided air-to-surface weapons as compared to the basic versions. Retaining the dogfighting potential of the standard *Fulcrum*, the aircraft acquires a strike potential comparable to that of the latest Western fighters, such as the Lockheed Martin F-16C Block 50 Fighting Falcon, Boeing F/A-18E/F Super Hornet, Dassault Mirage 2000-5 and Dassault Rafale C Mk 2.

The second basic package involves an increase in fuel capacity (both internal and external) and other refinements to the fuel system, as well as the installation of an in-flight refuelling system compatible with both Russian and Western tanker aircraft.

The third package deals with the fighter's avionics. This gives the fighter a completely new data presentation and control environment featuring full-colour multi-function liquid-crystal displays. The state-of-the-art flight instrumentation and navigation suite includes a satellite navigation module and is fully compliant to NATO and ICAO standards, which makes the MiG-29SMT more attractive for foreign customers and facilitates long-range flights outside Russia.

In its *izdeliye* 9.18 form the MiG-29SMT has the WCS and the navigation system united into the OPrNK-29SM integrated opto-electronic navigation/attack suite (**opt**iko-elek**tron**nyy prit**sel**'no-navigatsi**on**nyy **kom**pleks); a version of this suite designated

Above: The cockpit of MiG-29SMT '777 Green' (formerly '777 Blue', c/n 2960535403, f/n 4711) seen at the 2005 Dubai Air Show. The two MFDs are clearly visible.

This view of MiG-29SMT '777 Green' illustrates the altered fuselage spine housing a 950-litre fuel tank (one of the two dorsal tanks fitted to the *izdeliye* 9.17). This aircraft represents a cross-breed between the 9.17 and the basic *izdeliye* 9.12 as far as the airframe and fuel system are concerned.

Another view of MiG-29SMT '777 Green' at Dubai with various business jets and an Embraer EMB-145AEW in the background. The hastily modified spine has made this particular aircraft really ungainly, and the yucky 'swamp monster' camouflage does not help either!

OPrNK-29SMU has been developed for the MiG-29UBT, should there be a demand for this two-seat combat aircraft. This suite, which enables the fighter to navigate safely and use its air-to-air and air-to-surface weapons throughout its designated combat envelope, was developed by the Ramenskoye Instrument Design Bureau (RPKB – *Ramenskoye priborostroitel'noye konstrooktorskoye byuro*) headed by Givi I. Djandjgava. The SAU-451-05SMT automatic flight control system (*sistema avtomaticheskovo oopravleniya*) for the MiG-29SMT (*izdeliye* 9.18) and its SAU-451-05UBT version for the MiG-29UBT were jointly developed by the Elara Joint-Stock Co. from Cheboksary and MNPK Avionika ('Avionics' Moscow Scientific & Production Complex).

If the customer goes for a 'full option' upgrade, the MiG-29SMT becomes a Generation 4+ fighter whose combat potential closely matches that of the MiG-29M and the best Western fighters – in fact, it surpasses them in some respects. Such an aircraft will remain highly effective and hence competitive on the world market for the next 20 years.

Importantly, RSK MiG is prepared to perform the upgrade entirely on the customer's home ground, using the customer's own facilities. The corporation is currently performing MiG-29 upgrade work under contract with several nations; the first batches of *Fulcrums* upgraded to MiG-29SMT/MiG-29UBT stan-

dard have now been delivered to several foreign customers, including Yemen.

Notwithstanding the fact that the number of MiG-29 units in the Russian Air Force is declining by the year and a large number of early-production MiG-29s (mostly *Fulcrum-As* and MiG-29UBs) have been consigned to storage depots in Lipetsk and elsewhere, the Russian Air Force top command is showing an interest in having the *Fulcrum-Cs* (*izdeliye* 9.13) and MiG-29Ss (*izdeliye* 9.13S) updated to MiG-29SMT standard. Most of the design features that have been mastered in the course of upgrade work for foreign customers will probably be incorporated on the Russian Air Force's MiG-29SMTs, reducing the modernisation time and cutting costs.

Among other things, three aircraft sharing the MiG-29SMT designation but upgraded in different years and differing in avionics fit and systems/structural design were used both in the MiG-29SMT programme and in the reborn MiG-29K/MiG-29KUB programme described later; these were '917 Blue' (c/n 2960535400, fuselage number 4710), '777 Blue' (c/n 2960535403, f/n 4711) and '918 White' (c/n 2960536050, f/n 4815). By August 2005 '917 Blue' had been repainted in a rather shocking blue/violet splinter camouflage scheme with stylised 'MiG' titles on the fins for the MAKS-2005 airshow but the systems and structure remained unchanged since the late 1990s – the grossly bulged fuselage spine

housing additional fuel tankage was retained. This aircraft served as a testbed for certain systems and avionics components. In contrast, '918 White' (which basically matches the current specification of *izdeliye* 9.18) has an identical detachable semi-retractable IFR probe but retains the concave upper fuselage contour of the *izdeliye* 9.12 from which it was converted. Likewise sporting a splinter scheme (this time in sand/brown 'desert' colours), the aircraft was displayed at several international airshows, including MAKS-2003. For a while '918 White' was flown by the pilots of the 929th GLITs; as such it was among the static exhibits at Vladimirovka AB during the festivities on occasion of the Centre's 85th anniversary on 21st September 2005, being displayed with a full weapons load.

'777 Blue' initially had the systems updated to *izdeliye* 9.18 configuration (this included avionics standardised with those of the new-generation *Fulcrum* versions and the detachable IFR probe). Thus it was outwardly identical to '918 White' for a while, except for the paint job. In this guise the aircraft completed the opening stage of the trials. Then in early November 2005 it was retrofitted with a 950-litre (209 Imp gal) fuel tank aft of the cockpit, which gave it a singularly ungainly humpbacked appearance (the aircraft looked like a cross-breed between the *izdeliye* 9.12 and the *izdeliye* 9.17) and gained a three-tone green/grey camouflage for the Dubai 2005 airshow, where it was displayed statically as '777 Green' together with '918 White', which was in the flying display; thus MiG-29SMT c/n 2960535403 came to represent the finalised baseline configuration of *izdeliye* 9.18.

As already mentioned, the MiG-29SMT prototypes were primarily avionics testbeds (in particular, they were used to verify the central data processing system, the INS and the MFDs); the avionics fit was largely identical to that of the MiG-29K/KUB and MiG-29M/M2. Additionally, the State Research Institute for Aircraft Systems (GosNII AS) built a special test rig for integrating the avionics and armament of the *izdeliye* 9.18.

RSK MiG has now begun certification trials of the MiG-29SMT jointly with the Russian Air Force. Several versions of the national defence budget for 2006 are under consideration as of this writing, and all of them envisage upgrading the existing MiG-29 fleet. The number of aircraft to be upgraded depends on which version of the budget is endorsed by the State Duma (Parliament); what is certain, however, is that a substantial number of MiG-29s will be modernised, not just a handful of fighters for show purposes, which will give the Russian Air Force a tangible improvement in combat capability. The Air Force is due to place its initial order for the upgrade of operational *Fulcrums* to the current MiG-29SMT standard in 2006.

The upgrade increases the basic MiG-29's combat potential (especially in air-to-ground mode) 2.5 times. By the time MiG-29SMT '918 White' made its airshow appearance at Zhukovskiy RSK MiG had completed live weapons tests involving the use of precision-guided munitions – Kh-31A active radar homing anti-shipping missiles, Kh-31P anti-radiation missiles, Kh-29T TV-guided missiles and KAB-500Kr 'smart bombs' – with this aircraft at the 929th GLITs. Vladimir I. Barkovskiy, Director of the corporation's Engineering Centre, says the tests showed that the MiG-29SMT's new navigation suite developed by RPKB has significantly improved targeting accuracy with all types of unguided air-to-surface weapons.

In its current guise the MiG-29SMT has also attracted considerable interest on the part of some third-world countries. Yemen became the launch customer, placing an order for a batch of the upgraded fighters in 2003 (which is why MiG-29SMT '918 White' is sometimes referred to as 'the Yemeni version' because of its 'African' camouflage). RSK MiG continues its efforts to market the fighter in other parts of the world. At least one more export order for the MiG-29SMT is due to be signed by the end of 2005, says Barkovskiy, and two more nations may introduce this version in 2006.

MiG-29M Single-Seat Multi-Role Fighter (*izdeliye* 9.61)
MiG-29M2 Two-Seat Multi-Role Fighter (*izdeliye* 9.67)

In the late 1970s the Mikoyan Design Bureau started work on a radically improved version of the MiG-29. Designated MiG-29M (*modifitseerovannyy* – modified) or *izdeliye* 9.15, the aircraft had a considerably redesigned airframe, uprated engines, new avionics and deadlier weapons. Six prototypes were built, the first of which entered flight test on 25th April 1986. Stage 1 of the test programme was completed in September 1991; however, the programme was suspended in September 1993. This suspension was due to political upheavals and financial troubles.

Recently, however, the MiG-29M designation has been reallocated to a new member of the *Fulcrum* family. The management and top design staff of RSK MiG regard the 'new' MiG-29M and its MiG-29M2 derivative as the new generation of the *Fulcrum*'s land-based versions. As of now, approximately 1,500 copies of the 'first-generation' MiG-29 (*Fulcrum-A/C* and MiG-29UB) have been produced; whereas the MiG-29SMT (*izdeliye* 9.18) is regarded as the principal upgrade standard of today for existing aircraft, the MiG-29M and the MiG-29M2 are set to be the next new-production models. If enough orders are accumulated to resume MiG-29

The MiG-29M2 prototype ('154 White') was converted from the fourth prototype MiG-29M (*izdeliye* 9.15) whose tactical code it retains. Other giveaways are the dogtooth on the stabilator leading edge, the IFR probe and the fairing between the engine nozzles. The lightning bolt on the fin is a stylised 'MiG' inscription.

Above: The MiG-29M2 is seen with some of its weapons. Front row, left to right: the R-73, R-77, R-27R and R-27T AAMs, the Kh-35 anti-shipping missile, cannon ammunition, the Kh-29T air-to-surface missile and the same AAMs. Next are B-8M rocket pods; the aircraft carries Kh-31A ASMs and KAB-500T guided bombs.

Landing gear just beginning to retract, the MiG-29M2 pulls up into a sharp climb as it begins an aerobatics display at the MAKS-2005 airshow. Most of the pylons have been removed, except the outermost ones which carry the smoke generator pods.

Afterburners blazing, the MiG-29M2 completes a vertical climb at the MAKS-2001 airshow where it was unveiled. Note the original 'MRCA' titles and Russian flag bands on the tails.

production, the first MiG-29Ms and MiG-29M2s will roll off the line within a few years.

The single-seat MiG-29M (which, in its new guise, received the new in-house designation *izdeliye* 9.61) and the two-seat MiG-29M2 (*izdeliye* 9.67) are designed with the maximum possible degree of structural, avionics and armament commonality. Both versions have an identical forward fuselage which looks like a cross-breed between the MiG-29 *sans suffixe* (*Fulcrum-A/C*) and the MiG-29UB, combining the latter's tandem cockpits enclosed by a common aft-hinged canopy with a 'normal' large radome. The pilots sit on Zvezda K-36D-3.5 zero-zero ejection seats which create a vertical G load no higher than 3.5 during ejection and thus reduce the risk of spinal injuries without compromising safety. The workload distribution between the crewmembers of the MiG-29M2 ('front seat flies, back seat fires') enhances the aircraft's combat efficiency during strike/seek-and-destroy missions. On the

single-seater the rear cockpit is occupied by a 630-litre (138.6 Imp gal) auxiliary fuel tank.

Like the original MiG-29M (*izdeliye* 9.15), the aircraft has traded the forward air intake blocker doors and spring-loaded dorsal doors for foreign object damage (FOD) prevention grilles further downstream. This frees up internal space inside the LERXes, allowing it to be used for additional fuel. Another feature retained from the original MiG-29M is the fully-retractable L-shaped IFR probe on the port side of the nose in line with the cockpit windshield.

The aircraft will be powered by the new RD-33MK afterburning turbofan developed by NPO Klimov in St. Petersburg. The RD-33MK is a derivative of the production RD-33 Srs 3 powering the MiG-29SE and the MiG-29SMT. Apart from the addition of full authority digital engine control (FADEC), the RD-33MK features revisions to the low-pressure and high-pressure compressors, the combustion chamber and the HP and LP turbines. The

overall effect of these changes increases the thrust in full afterburner to 9,000 kgp (19,840 lbst) and at full military power to 5,400 kgp (11,905 lbst). The use of a smokeless combustion chamber has helped to address a perennial problem – the RD-33's high smoke signature. Also, the RD-33MK's designated service life is doubled to 4,000 hours.

NPO Klimov has also developed the all-new KSA-33M accessory gearbox. As distinct from the KSA-2 and KSA-3 accessory gearboxes fitted to earlier versions of the MiG-29, it consists of two independent sections powered by the respective engines, each with its own set of generators and pumps and carrying its own auxiliary power unit (APU). This significantly enhances reliability and operating efficiency in extreme climates. The new Klimov VK-100 APU is an uprated derivative of the GTDE-117 used hitherto. Unlike previous versions of the MiG-29, the APU exhausts are located dorsally.

The MiG-29M/M2 will be able to fulfil air defence/air superiority, overland or maritime strike and reconnaissance missions, detecting, identifying and destroying well-protected aerial, ground and maritime targets in the daytime and at night, in any weather and in an ECM environment, operating singly or as part of a group. Importantly, the MiG-29M/M2 has considerable commonality with the MiG-29SMT (*izdeliye* 9.18) as regards avionics and armament. This means that most of the test flights performed by the MiG-29SMT and the MiG-29K (see later) will earn certification points for the MiG-29M/M2 as well, greatly speeding up the latter models' certification and production entry.

A few words need to be said about the systems and equipment of the MiG-29M/M2. The aircraft has a quadruplex fly-by-wire (FBW) control system. Currently the MiG-29M2 prototype retains the SDU-915-01 control system of the original MiG-29M. Later, when the intended RD-33MK engines with KLIVT vectoring nozzles are fitted, the MiG-29M/M2 will feature the SDU-915OVT control system (OVT = *otklonyayemyy vektor tyaghi* – thrust vector control) developed by MNPK Avionika jointly with the Elara JSC. The new version is augmented by a quadruply redundant digital processor responsible, among other things, for controlling the vectoring nozzles; this makes for efficient control of the aircraft at minimum airspeeds and extreme angles of attack.

The avionics have an open architecture based on the MIL-STD-1553B digital databus, which allows avionics and weapons of non-Russian origin to be integrated at the customer's demand. The new fighter family's WCS includes a new N011M Bars (Leopard) multi-mode radar with air-to-air, air-to-surface and ground mapping modes (developed by

NIIP – the Moscow Institute of Instrument Engineering named after Viktor V. Tikhomirov), a new infra-red search & track/laser ranger unit and a helmet-mounted sight.

The new IRST/LR unit offers high performance and is capable of detecting aerial targets in both head-on and pursuit mode. The laser rangefinder/target designator can be used against aerial and ground targets alike. The helmet-mounted sight is likewise more advanced than the Shchel'-1UM (Crevice-1UM) used hitherto; it provides target information to the missiles' seeker heads and projects flight/navigation and target information right into the pilot's eyes.

The data presentation system features a ShKAI wide-angle monochrome HUD and three (or, on the MiG-29M2, seven) MFI 10-7 high-performance 6x8" (152x203 mm) liquid-crystal MFDs framed by function keys. In addition to the primary flight instrument mode the system can display a digital terrain map and tactical situation data, allowing the pilot to maintain situational awareness and use his weapons effectively.

The navigation/attack suite of the MiG-29M/MiG-29M2 incorporates ring laser gyros and built-in satellite navigation receivers, as well as radio navigation aids and other equipment enabling quick and accurate positioning and computation of the aircraft's motion parameters, the data being fed to relevant systems. A mission profile prepared personally by the pilot on a to computer can be uploaded from a flash card; the digital map saved in the profile will be displayed on the MFDs. The communications suite comprises a UHF radio and

a VHF radio, one of which can operate in data link mode. The integrated ECM/ESM suite includes a radar homing and warning system, an active jammer, a missile warning system (MWS), a laser illumination warning system and chaff/flare dispensers.

The fighter is armed with a 30-mm (1.18 calibre) GSh-301 fast-firing cannon and has eight underwing weapons hardpoints plus a centreline hardpoint which can likewise be used for carrying bombs. The two inboard pylons under each wing can be fitted with tandem bomb racks, effectively increasing the number of hardpoints to 13. Air-to-air weapons include the R-77 (RVV-AE) active radar homing medium-range missile and the R-73E short-range AAM. For anti-shipping strike missions the aircraft can carry Kh-31A and Kh-35E active radar homing missiles; the Kh-31P passive radar homing variety is used for destroying enemy radars. Pinpoint strikes against ground targets are made possible by Kh-29T TV-guided missiles and KAB-500Kr TV-guided bombs. The unguided weapons include ordinary and cluster bombs of up to 500 kg (1,102 lb) calibre (up to eleven 500-kg bombs can be carried), 240-mm (9.44-in) S-24B heavy unguided rockets (up to six) and 80-mm (3.14-in) S-8KOM folding-fin aircraft rockets (FFARs) in up to six 20-round B-8M1 pods. The maximum ordnance load is 5,500 kg (12,125 lb).

The combat radius of the new fighter family is considerably greater than the standard *Fulcrum-A/C*'s thanks to the increased internal and external fuel capacity and the provision of IFR capability. The IFR probe is

compatible with Russian and Western tankers alike. The aircraft will also have 'buddy' refuelling capability. The MiG-29M/M2's range on internal/external fuel (unrefuelled) is estimated as 1,650-1,800 km (1,024-1,118 miles).

The cumulative effect of these design changes increases the MiG-29M/M2's combat potential over the *Fulcrum-A/C* by a factor of 2.5-3.5 in strike mode and 1.7-1.8 in air-to-air mode.

The MiG-29M2 prototype ('154 White') was converted from the fourth prototype MiG-29M/*izdeliye* 9.15 ('154 Blue', c/n 2960905554) by grafting a MiG-29UB cockpit section onto the former single-seater. The machine made its public debut at the MAKS-2001 airshow on 14th-19th August 2001.

The Russian Air Force could theoretically order the MiG-29M/M2, given the proper funding. However, a number of traditional export customers are far more likely to order it – first and foremost India. The Indian Air Force is currently running an ambitious programme called Multi-Role Combat Aircraft (MRCA). It envisages the purchase and licence production of a total of 126 modern multi-role fighters to supplant the MiG-23MF and complement the MiG-29 and Mirage 2000N. In the IAF's prospective three-tier structure the MRCA is to occupy a position between the HAL LCA light combat aircraft and the upgraded MiG-21*bis* (at the lower end of the scale) and the heavy Su-30MKI. Hence the Indian Ministry of Defence is to hold a tender under the MRCA programme. At the Aero India 2005 airshow, RSK MiG announced its plans to submit the MiG-29M/M2 for the

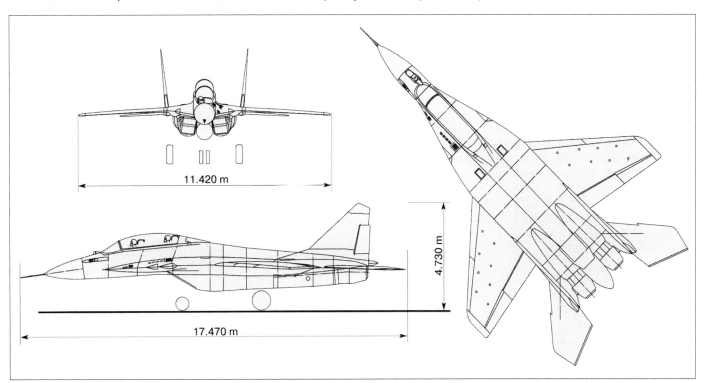

11.420 m

4.730 m

17.470 m

A three-view of the MiG-29M2. The production MiG-29M will have an identical airframe and a fuel tank occupying the rear cockpit.

Indian tender. Both versions are to enter production towards the end of the decade. Later, at the MAKS-2005 airshow, RSK MIG General Director Aleksey Fyodorov said that the version submitted for the Indian tender would be called MiG-35. No details of the fighter's systems and equipment were disclosed, except that the MiG-35 will be powered by the thrust-vectoring version of the RD-33MK.

MiG-29K Single-Seat Shipboard Fighter (*izdeliye* 9.41)
MiG-29KUB Two-Seat Shipboard Fighter (*izdeliye* 9.47)

On 20th January 2004 Russia and India signed a contract worth more than US$ 700 million. Under this contract RSK MiG was to deliver twelve MiG-29K single-seat shipboard fighters and four MiG-29KUB combat trainers to the Indian Navy; these aircraft were to form the carrier wing of India's first CTOL aircraft carrier. The contract also includes the training of the customer's personnel, the delivery and commissioning of flight simulators, spares supplies and the organisation of maintenance at the customer's facilities. Deliveries are to take place in 2007-09 and the Indian Navy holds an option for a further 30 MiG-29K/KUBs to be delivered in 2010-2015. The fighters will operate from the aircraft carrier INS *Vikramaditya* (formerly RNS *Admiral Gorshkov*) which will be extensively converted to enable CTOL operations; this involves installation of a ski jump, among other things.

Now we come to the most important bit. Despite sharing the MiG-29K designation of the shipboard fighter developed for the Soviet Navy and known at RSK MiG as *izdeliye* 9.31, the multi-role aircraft being developed under the Indian contract is rather different. The design staff of RSK MiG has gone to great lengths to adapt the fighter to the Indian Navy's requirements and to the new ship from which the MiG-29K will operate, incorporating the latest features of the MiG-29 family's development.

Two versions are being developed in parallel: the MiG-29K single-seat multi-role fighter (which, in its new guise, received the new in-house designation *izdeliye* 9.41) and the two-seat MiG-29KUB (*izdeliye* 9.47) which could be used both as a fighter and as a combat-capable trainer. To save time and cut costs the two versions will have more than 90% commonality as regards the airframe and systems and nearly 100% commonality as regards avionics and armament; in other words, basically the MiG-29K differs from the MiG-29KUB only in having an extra fuel tank occupying the rear cockpit.

The shipboard MiG-29K/KUB will have maximum possible structural and systems/equipment commonality with the land-based MiG-29M/M2. In other words, implementation of this programme will result in a unique quartet of Generation 4+ combat aircraft (the MiG-29K/KUB and the MiG-29M/M2) having 90% commonality. This approach offers important advantages, cutting production costs (and hence the flyaway price), simplifying operational procedures (including flight and ground crew training), facilitating spares procurement and streamlining the operator's fleet. This, together with the high flight performance and combat potential, makes the new-generation MiG-29 family a strong player on the world fighter market.

The principal differences between the MiG-29M/M2 and the MiG-29K/KUB is that the latter incorporates features associated with carrier operations – folding wings, a reinforced landing gear optimised for no-flare landings and an arrester hook. The wings of the MiG-29K (*izdeliye* 9.41) and MiG-29KUB are broadly similar to those of the MiG-29K (*izdeliye* 9.31) as regards planform, span, airfoils, the wing-folding mechanism, the configuration of the integral fuel tanks and the number of external stores hardpoints. The main differences lie in the high-lift devices. The double-slotted trailing-edge flaps feature increased chord and area, protruding beyond the trailing edge when retracted. The simple leading-edge flaps are replaced by double-hinged ones and their maximum deflection is increased from 20° to 30°; the LE flaps are now continuously controlled by the aircraft's flight control system, deploying automatically to the required angle in concert with the ailerons and stabilators in accordance with the current AOA and Mach number.

Additional vortex flaps are installed on the underside of the leading-edge root extensions. These are strictly landing devices; on take-off and in cruise mode they are retracted flush with the underside of the LERXes. As they deploy during landing approach, they generate additional vortices, enhancing lift and reducing dangerous fore-and-aft oscillations. The changes to the high-lift devices are to improve the MiG-29K/KUB's manoeuvrability and enhance flight safety during approach and landing.

The MiG-29K/KUB fills the following basic roles:
• air defence of carrier task forces and interception of aerial targets flying at 20-27,000 m (65-88,580 ft) and speeds up to 2,500-2,700 km/h (1,552-1,677 mph) in any weather, day or night;
• destruction of enemy air assets in areas where 'friendly' submarines are in operation;
• anti-shipping strikes and strikes against ground targets, using both precision-guided munitions and unguided weapons;
• destruction of anti-assault pillboxes on the coastline and providing close air support (CAS) to assault groups;

• support and protection of other (shore-based) naval aircraft en route to and from the battle area;
• reconnaissance.

In addition, the two-seat MiG-29KUB can be used for proficiency training and conversion training for the single-seat MiG-29K. If a specially developed PAZ-1MK 'buddy' refuelling pod is fitted, the MiG-29K/KUB can refuel probe-equipped sister aircraft, extending their range and endurance.

Unlike the MiG-29M/M2, the shipboard versions have a new KSU-941 quadruplex digital FBW control system developed by MNPK Avionika and Elara. It is based on the programmable FBW control system developed for the MiG-AT advanced trainer.

Since the MiG-29K/KUB will operate in a salty oceanic environment, special corrosion protection measures for the airframe, avionics/equipment and engines will be taken. Radar-absorbing material coatings will reduce the fighter's radar cross-section by a factor of 4 to 5 as compared to the standard MiG-29.

The Indian Navy versions will be powered by RD-33MK engines and equipped with the associated KSA-33M accessory gearbox and VK-100s APUs. The dorsally located APU exhausts reduce the fire hazard during carrier operations and enable the carriage of a new enlarged centreline drop tank.

The internal fuel capacity of the MiG-29K (*izdeliye* 9.41) is more than 50% greater than the basic MiG-29's and more than 16% greater than that of the original MiG-29K (*izdeliye* 9.31). The increase is due to the provision of additional fuselage tanks (including a 500-litre (110 Imp gal) tank in the fuselage spine and smaller tanks in the LERXes) and the installation of a 630-litre (138.6 Imp gal) auxiliary tank occupying the rear cockpit; this latter tank is omitted on the MiG-29KUB. Additionally, the capacity of the centreline drop tank has been increased from 1,250 litres (275 Imp gal) to 2,150 litres (473 Imp gal) and the number of underwing drop tanks holding 1,150 litres (253 Imp gal) each has been increased from two to four.

As compared to its *izdeliye* 9.31 namesake the avionics fit of the MiG-29K (*izdeliye* 9.41) is at least 80% new and has considerable commonality with the production-standard MiG-29SMT (*izdeliye* 9.18). In response to the Indian Navy's wishes the MiG-29K/KUB will feature several avionics items of Indian and French origin. The PrNK-29K and PrNK-29KUB navigation/attack suites developed for the MiG-29K and MiG-29KUB respectively permit navigation and engagement of aerial and ground/surface targets throughout the aircraft's designated combat envelope, singly or as part of a group. The avionics have an open (modular) architecture based on the MIL-STD-1553B digital databus.

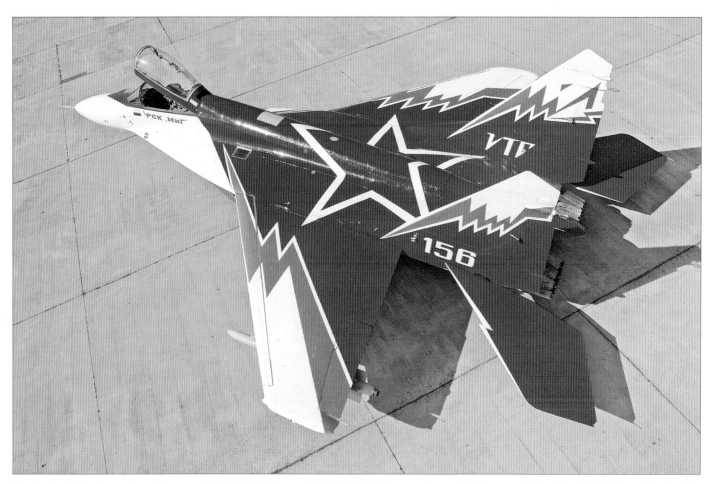

Resplendent in its show colours, the super-agile MiG-29OVT demonstrator ('156 White') was again converted from one of the original MiG-29Ms and likewise wears 'lightning-style' 'MiG' titles on the tails (in Cyrillic and Roman script). The 'VTC' on the starboard fin stands for 'vectoring thrust control'.

The suite is built around a digital data processing system which, like the three principal targeting systems – the Zhuk-ME radar developed by the Fazotron-NIIR corporation, the IRST/LR and the system downloading target information to the passive seeker heads of the anti-radiation missiles – is Russian-made. Other systems, like the helmet-mounted sight, are of foreign origin.

The aircraft's 'nervous system' comprises four multiplex databuses, which considerably speeds up communication between the miscellaneous electronic systems and increases its reliability. For the first time on a Russian aircraft the data transmission rate conforms to the toughest existing standard (fibre channel); copper wires are used as of now, but fibre-optic cables will be incorporated later.

The armament of the MiG-29K/KUB is identical to that of the MiG-29M/M2, including the ability to carry Kh-31A and Kh-35E anti-shipping missiles. Guided and unguided weapons of non-Russian origin may be integrated at the customer's demand.

The MiG-29K (*izdeliye* 9.41) and the MiG-29KUB (*izdeliye* 9.47) will be capable of day/night, all-weather, year-round operation in any climate, including tropics with ambient temperatures up to +35°C (+95°F) and air humidity up to 100%. The aircraft will be able

to operate singly or in groups in the face of enemy fighter opposition and in an ECM environment, operating from CTOL carriers equipped with a ski jump or from shore bases. The take-off run on a carrier deck equipped with a bow ski jump is estimated as 125-195 m (410-640 ft).

As compared to existing MiG-29 variants the Indian Navy versions will have a longer designated service life and lower operating costs (due to being operated on a 'technical condition' basis with no rigidly set overhaul intervals). This cuts operating costs per flight hour by nearly 40%.

The first manufacturing drawings of the 'new' MiG-29K were issued in the autumn of 1999 and the first metal was cut immediately. By early 2005 two prototypes had reached an advanced stage of construction. The first prototype MiG-29KUB is expected to enter flight test in December 2005 or early 2006, the single-seat MiG-29K (*izdeliye* 9.41) following in the spring of 2006.

MiG-29OVT Development Aircraft

The highlights of the MAKS-2005 airshow included a breathtaking flying display by a development aircraft presented by RSK MiG – the MiG-29OVT experimental super-agile multi-role fighter flown by the corporation's

chief test pilot Pavel N. Vlasov. The aircraft, which had been converted from the final prototype of the MiG-29M (*izdeliye* 9.15) – in effect, a pre-production example, – was really a propulsion testbed meant to verify a version of the RD-33 engine fitted with an all-aspect vectoring nozzle. In other words, '156 White' was a TVC technology demonstrator – or a control configured vehicle (CCV).

The story began in the mid-1990s when NPO Klimov commenced development of its own TVC concept as an answer to the rival Lyul'ka-Saturn design bureau's AL-31FP thrust-vectoring afterburning turbofan created for the Su-27 family. NPO Klimov's vectoring nozzle was intended for light fighters and branded KLIVT (*Klimovskiy vektor tyaghi* or Klimov's Vectoring Thrust). After analysing the TVC research undertaken in the Soviet Union and abroad, the engineers of NPO Klimov concluded that the best option was to deflect the nozzle's supersonic section (the petals). This not only made the design simpler and lighter but also reduced the deflection time and, most importantly, allowed the nozzle petals to move in any direction. All the petals of the supersonic section were deflected at the required angle simultaneously, the motion being imparted via push-pull rods from a single control ring; this, in

Above: The MiG-29OVT makes one of its thrilling demonstrations at the MAKS-2005 airshow. Here it is seen lighting up its afterburners as it recovers from a flat spin (note the direction of the smoke trails).

Blue', c/n 2960905556) finally received a shipset of flight-cleared RD-133s, making its first post-conversion flight as '156 White' in August 2003 with test pilot Pavel Vlasov at the controls.

By early August 2005 RSK MiG test pilots Pavel Vlasov and Mikhail Belyayev had made more than 50 flights in '156 White' in which the TVC system was put through its paces and its integration with the FBW control system was verified. This prompted the decision to demonstrate the aircraft at the MAKS-2005 airshow. Those who witnessed the aircraft's demonstration flights at the show said the MiG-29OVT was at least equal, or maybe even superior, in manoeuvrability to the super-agile Su-30MKI which had by then become a regular airshow performer; the aircraft could do loops and spirals literally around its own nose. However, there's more to it than just spectacular and unique aerobatics at an airshow; RSK MiG Chief Designer Nikolay N. Boontin, who is in charge of the MiG-29K/KUB, MiG-29M/M2 and MiG-29OVT programmes, says that all-aspect TVC endows the new MiG with entirely new capabilities both in normal flight modes and in superagility mode.

In the course of its research into thrust vectoring control NPO Klimov came to the conclusion that the design of the KLIVT nozzle can be adapted to other engine types, including Western ones. The MiG-29M/M2 and its derivatives with TVC may find a market both in Russia and abroad; among other things, the thrust-vectoring MiG-35 has been entered for the Indian Air Force's MRCA tender.

turn, was powered by three hydraulic actuators located at equal intervals on a fixed ring running around the afterburner. The thrust vectoring angles were ±15° in all directions; the maximum deflection speed was eventually increased from 30°/sec to 60°/sec.

Concurrently the engine was to receive a new FADEC system and be uprated from 5,040 to 5,600 kgp (from 11,110 to 12,345 lbst) at full military power and from 8,300 to 9,000 kgp (from 18,300 to 19,840 lbst) in full

afterburner. In this guise the engine was initially known as the RD-133; later, however, the RD-133 designation was dropped, the engine being referred to simply as the 'thrust-vectoring RD-33'.

The first prototype of the KLIVT nozzle was completed by early 1997. Flight tests of the thrust-vectoring engine on a suitably modified MiG-29 were due to commence in late 1997, but financial problems delayed this until 2003. That year the sixth prototype MiG-29M ('156

The MiG-29OVT is powered by thrust-vectoring engines whose obvious identification features are the three TVC actuator fairings located around the nozzle. The IRST and the IFR probe were deleted in the course of the conversion.

Chapter 3

Yak-130

Russia's New Trainer

At the end of the 1980s the Soviet Air Force took the decision to write a new set of general operational requirements (GOR) for a dedicated training aircraft, provisionally known simply as the UTS (*oochebno-trenirovochnyy samolyot* – conversion/proficiency trainer). The GOR was issued to a number of design bureaux that were called upon to respond to the requirements.

In the early 1990s, four Russian design bureaux – Mikoyan, Myasishchev, Sukhoi and Yakovlev – took up the challenge and set to work on their individual proposals for a new-generation trainer design. In contrast to the practices of the Soviet period when such undertakings were generously funded by the state, budgetary constraints associated with *perestroika* compelled the design bureaux to finance the project design work out of their own resources. An important aspect of the competition was its open character, whereby foreign partners were to be invited to participate in a joint project with the winning contender. The first round of the contest resulted in the Sukhoi and Myasishchev designs being eliminated from the shortlist, the Yakovlev Yak-130 and Mikoyan MiG-AT projects being chosen for the further work. In both cases, prototypes were built and much effort was spent on winning the support from prospective customers both at home and abroad so as to ensure future sales. Eventually the Russian Air Force selected the Yak-130, but more about that later.

When designing the Yak-130, the project team considered the fact that it would have to train pilots both for existing fighter types and for future fifth-generation fighters offering considerably better performance and greater agility than contemporary aircraft. It was decided to utilise an integral (blended wing/body) layout with swept wings and engines offering a comparatively high thrust-to-weight ratio, with the intention to emulate as closely as possible the subsonic manoeuvring characteristics of the newer fighters.

The Yak-130 emerged as a subsonic two-seater with mid-set cropped-delta wings having 31° leading-edge sweep outside of the large curved LERXes which, together with full-span leading-edge slats, were to permit controlled flight at an angle of attack up to 35°. The wings were initially fitted with tall winglets.

The slab stabilisers repeated the wing planform and featured anhedral and a large dogtooth (omitted on the first prototype). The vertical tail was swept. The cockpit was equipped with two Zvezda K-36 zero-zero ejection seats, which were sharply stepped to ensure good visibility for the instructor. They were enclosed by a large sideways-opening canopy supplemented by a single-curvature frameless windscreen.

The aircraft was originally intended to be powered by two Ivchenko AI-25TL turbofans, but these were soon changed to the more modern DV-2 turbofans. The DV-2 was origi-

Above: An early desktop model of the Yak-130 advanced trainer marked Yak-UTK (Yak Training System); note the winglets and the unbroken stabilator leading edge.

Another model featuring weapons pylons and a dogtooth on the stabilator leading edge.

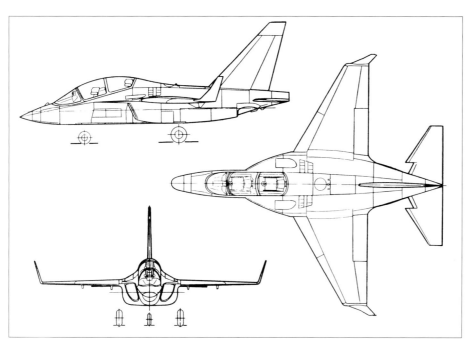

Above: An early three-view of the Yak-130 trainer. Note the auxiliary air intakes in the LERXes which open on the ground when the main air intakes are closed by FOD prevention blocker doors.

Above: Originally known simply as the Yak-130, the first prototype is seen here at the Yakovlev Corporation's experimental plant in Yakovlev/Aermacchi demonstrator colours with the exhibit code 296.

The still unregistered Yak-130 in an early test flight, showing the original winglets. These were later removed, the machine was registered RA-43130 and rebranded Yak-130D (for Demonstrator).

nally developed as a Soviet-Czechoslovak co-operation programme and later as a joint project between the Progress Engine Design Bureau (the Ukraine) and the Považske Strojarne enterprise (Slovakia); hence the DV initials standing for 'Dnepr-Vltava', the names of the two rivers on which the two enterprises are located. Actually, the model intended for installation in the production Yak-130 was the RD-35M, a version of the DV-2 modified by NPO Klimov and rated at 2,200 kgp (4,850 lbst). At a still later stage this engine, in turn, gave place to the Ivchenko (ZMKB Progress) AI-222-25 turbofans (see below).

A curious feature of the Yak-130, which it shares with the Mikoyan MiG-29 fighter, is the provision of blocker doors which close the air intakes completely when the engines are run on the ground to prevent FOD. When they are closed, the engines draw air through dorsal auxiliary intakes in the LERXes closed by mechanically-linked doors. Unlike the MiG-29, the blocker doors remain closed in flight with the landing gear down, opening (and the auxiliary upper intakes closing) as the gear retracts.

Originally it was planned to build the Yak-130 as a joint venture with Aermacchi of Italy, with which Yakovlev entered a partnership in 1994. Aermacchi shared design and production rights and had exclusive marketing rights outside the former Soviet Union. However, as a result of differing time scales and priorities, Aermacchi eventually took a decision to develop the concept independently as the Aermacchi M-346, leaving the Russian side to continue development work on the Yak-130 design on its own.

The main Russian participant in the Yak-130 programme, apart from the Yakovlev Corporation itself, is the Sokol (Falcon) aircraft factory in Nizhniy Novgorod; on the engine side, it was the NPO Klimov State Engine Manufacturing Enterprise of St Petersburg, but at present this role has passed to Moscow-based MMPP Salyut as the prospective supplier of the AI-222-25 engines.

In August 2003, during the MAKS-2003 air show, an agreement was signed on the merger of the Yakovlev Design Bureau and the Irkut Aircraft Corporation. The Yakovlev people hope that this merger will facilitate the promotion of the Yak-130 in foreign markets as a useful supplement to its deliveries to the Russian Air Force, which has selected it over the MiG-AT. The Yak-130 has a chance to win a niche on the Indian market where the Irkut Corporation has a foothold.

The Ukraine has voiced an intention to adopt the Yak-130 for its Air Force. On 14th May 2004 Ukrainian Air Force Commander-in-Chief Lieutenant-General Yaroslav Skal'ko said in a press interview that there were plans to use the Yak-130 for training Ukrainian military pilots and that assembly of these aircraft would be organised in Odessa. The Ukraine is participating in the Yak-130 programme as an engine supplier.

The first prototype Yak-130 was soon redesignated Yak-130D ('Demonstrator') – an appellation which it fully justified by taking part in various airshows in Russia and abroad. The Yak-130D left the assembly shop on 30th November 1994 and made its first flight on 25th April 1996, bearing the number 296 on the nose gear doors. Unlike the prototypes of previous Russian military aircraft, the Yak-130 sported a striking white/bluish grey/ red colour scheme in a decidedly civilian style with Yakovlev OKB and Aermacchi logos.

In its original configuration the Yak-130D featured winglets which soon proved to be insufficiently rigid and were removed. It had a characteristic flattened nose with chines. The slab stabilisers lacked the dogtooth which was envisaged by an early project configuration. The machine was demonstrated both with and without weapons pylons (three under each wing).

In December 1998 during routine test flying from the Aermacchi flight test facility at Venegono, Italy, the Yak-130D demonstrated one of the most important parameters expected of the new trainer, safe handling at critical angles of attack, by achieving an AoA of 42° in controlled and stabilised flight. This

Above: The Yak-130D in its ultimate configuration with no winglets and a wing leading edge dogtooth. The aircraft has been repainted in a three-tone camouflage scheme.

Despite wearing camouflage colours and the tactical code '091 White outline', the Yak-130D retains the civil registration RA-43130. Here it is seen carrying B-8M1 and B-13L FFAR pods and R-60M AAMs; arrayed on the ground are FAB-250M-62 bombs, UPK-23-250 cannon pods, KMGU submunitions pods and R-73 AAMs.

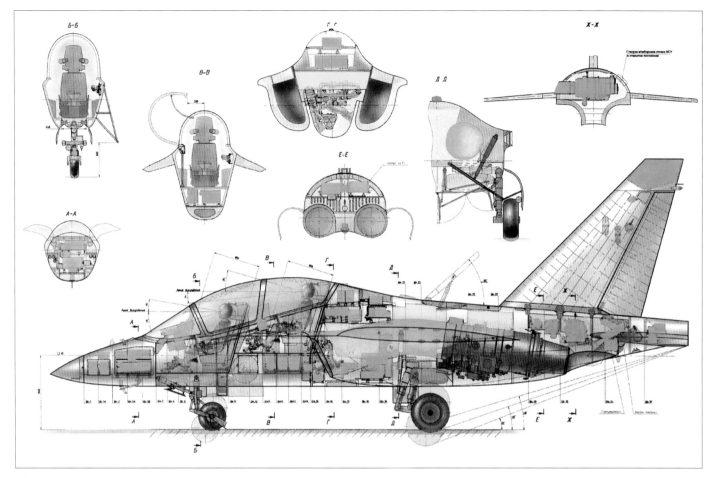

Above: This cutaway drawing represents the production version of the Yak-130 which is very different from the Yak-130D prototype in both shape and content. Note the nose radome.

The fuselage of the first production-standard Yak-130 takes shape at the Sokol plant in Nizhniy Novgorod. Note the lack of nose chines and the apertures for the dorsal air intakes in the LERXes.

was followed by several more high-alpha flights to validate the flight control system.

In August 1999 the machine was demonstrated with a number of modifications introduced in cooperation with Aermacchi and reflecting the suggestions made by Italian specialists. The winglets were gone, the wings acquired a dogtooth; small trapezoidal fences were added at the wing/LERX junctions and ahead of the windshield. The demonstrator was now registered RA-43130 and wore a revised colour scheme. After the dissolution of the partnership it was repainted in camouflage colours and retained only the Yak logo, receiving the tactical code '01 White outline' in addition to the civil registration. Another outward change was the addition of a heat shield aft of the APU outlet on the starboard side of the rear fuselage.

At a stage when the Yakovlev OKB and Aermacchi were still maintaining their partnership, their common plans envisaged starting the manufacture of a production version differing considerably from the Yak-130D (or Yak/AEM-130D) prototype. It would be an aircraft of smaller dimensions, its wing span being reduced from 11.25 m (36 ft 11 in) to 10.4 m (34 ft 1½ in), the fuselage length from 12.4 m (40 ft 8³⁄₁₆ in) to 11.24 m (36 ft 10½ in) and wing area reduced to 23.5 m² (253 sq ft).

To improve visibility, the nose would be drooped; the fuselage would be provided with a pointed tailcone and made shallower; the wheel base would be reduced. The DV-2 engines would give place to DV-2S turbofans with full-authority digital engine control (FADEC) and operational life improvements developed in conjunction with NPO Klimov and the Central Aero Engine Research Institute (TsIAM) in Russia as the RD-35. This version was known as the Yak/AEM-130S (*sereeynyy* – production, used attributively).

This project did not materialise in its original form; still, it provided the basis for later production versions developed separately by the Yakovlev OKB and the Aermacchi company (see below).

The first Russian production version of the Yak-130 embodies a considerable degree of redesign as compared to the Yak-130D prototype. The changes incorporated in this version reflect the somewhat changed concept of the Yak-130's employment in the Russian Air Force that emerged by the beginning of the 21st century. A new situation in the development of the Russian Air Force dictated the need to transform the Yak-130 from a pure trainer into a combat trainer capable of being used for practising up to 80% of the service pilots' entire training programme, as well as for live weapons training. Furthermore, the new threats to Russia's security are largely associated with a shift from all-out warfare to low-intensity local conflicts in which a modern combat trainer possessing a secondary attack capability is an effective and less costly alternative to using more potent and expensive combat aircraft.

The Yak-130 modified to meet the Russian Air Force's additional requirements should cope effectively with both training and combat tasks.

The production version differs outwardly from the Yak-130D in having a larger-diameter pointed ogival nose cone housing a radar, reshaped air intakes, a dogtooth stabiliser leading edge and wingtip launch rails for short-range AAMs. A conformal cannon pod can be fitted under the fuselage.

The combat trainer is powered by Ukrainian AI-222-25 turbofans developed by the Ivchenko 'Progress' Engine Design Bureau (ZMKB) and built by Motor Sich, both of Zaporozhye. The AI-222-25 delivering 2,500 kgp (5,510 lbst) for take-off will also be built for the Russian Air Force at the MMPP Salyut Moscow Engine Production Association in cooperation with Motor Sich. Thus it meets the key requirement posed by the Russian Air Force: its aircraft will be powered by engines of Russian manufacture (the Yak-130D prototype has Slovak-built DV-2 turbofans).

The production Yak-130's specifications include a take-off weight around nine tons

Above: Head-on view of the first production-standard Yak-130 with an impressive array of air-to-ground weapons, including precision-guided munitions. Note the wingtip missile rails.

(19,850 lb), a top speed of 1,060 km/h (659 mph), a service ceiling of 12,000 m (39,360 ft) and a range of 2,000 km (1,240 miles). The aircraft can carry up to three tons (6,610 lb) of external stores on nine hardpoints; these can accommodate essentially the whole range of weapons used by Russian tactical aircraft, including bombs of up to 500 kg (1,102 lb) calibre, unguided rockets and guided air-to-air and air-to-surface missiles. External stores may include TV- or laser-guided bombs like the KAB-500, Kh-25ML guided air-to-surface missiles, as well as foreign-made missiles like the AGM-65 Maverick or other weapons. Light armour will be provided to protect the cockpit, powerplant compartment and bays where the vital systems and equipment are installed. A mock-up of the production-model cockpit exhibited in 2001 sported a retractable in-flight refuelling probe on the starboard side ahead of the windshield.

The use of the Yak-130 for combat proficiency training does not necessarily involve real missile launches or bomb drops. The onboard system for simulating the weapons use mode ensures the possibility of simulating air combat, the firing of air-to-air missiles with IR- and radar-homing seeker heads, and the use of the ECM and IRCM systems; it can also simulate an attack against ground targets with the use of guided missiles and unguided rockets, as well as the use of guns.

During the initial stages of training the Yak-130 can be more 'forgiving' towards the errors committed by trainees which will enable them to master the essentials more quickly. When the pilots pass to further stages of training, including special flight modes and combat training, a special system for altering the flight control system software will make it possible to endow the Yak-130 with dynamic characteristics approximating those of the

The first production-standard aircraft, '01 White', with landing gear just beginning to retract. The production version 'gone on a diet' makes an interesting comparison with the Yak-130D on page 68.

Above: Yak-130 '01 White' in a test flight; note the low-visibility outline star insignia and the APU exhaust. Being painted matt dark green overall, the Yak-130 is pure frustration for photographers – the machine tends to appear as a black silhouette livened up only by the Day-Glo orange wing and fin tips.

This page and below left: Here, bright sunshine reveals the revised colours with normal red stars and the logo of the Sokol plant added on the rudder, as well as the dorsal auxiliary inlet grilles and wing and the stabilator… er… dogteeth. Note the FOD prevention doors and open dorsal intakes on the taxying aircraft.

Above: Still in primer finish and coded '02 Black' for the time being, the second production-standard Yak-130 runs up the engines at Nizhniy Novgorod-Sormovo. Note the radome and the dielectric fin cap.

Above: Negative and positive Yaks! Together, the first two machines make an interesting picture. Note how the canopy opens to starboard.

This view of '02 Black' shows the closed FOD prevention doors, the shape of the LERXes, the three hardpoints under each wing (plus wingtip missile rails) and the two-section flaps.

aircraft to be simulated – such as the MiG-29, Su-27 or Su-30. Theoretically any aircraft can be simulated, including the Boeing (McDonnell Douglas) F-15 Eagle, Lockheed Martin F-16 Fighting Falcon, Boeing (McDD) F/A-18 Hornet, Dassault Mirage 2000, Dassault Rafale, Eurofighter EF2000 Typhoon and the prospective American fifth-generation fighters, such as the Lockheed Martin F-35 (Joint Strike Fighter).

The first production-standard Yak-130 (confusingly, also coded '01 White' – albeit in solid digits this time) made its maiden flight from Nizhniy Novgorod-Sormovo on 30th April 2004 with Yakovlev OKB chief test pilot Roman P. Taskayev at the controls. Thus, this first production model of the Yak-130 powered by AI-222-25 turbofans started its flight development programme. The integrated test programme will span over two years. According to the present plans, the flight tests will involve four production machines.

The second machine (originally '02 Black', later repainted as '02 White') joined the test programme in the spring of 2005. It took to the air on 5th April, flown by Yakovlev OKB test pilots Vasiliy Sevast'yanov and Roman Taskayev. The testing of the third flight test example was due to begin in the autumn of 2005. The construction of this machine is fully funded by the Russian Air Force.

In February 2005 Russian Air Force Commander-in-Chief Army General Vladimir Mikhailov appointed a State commission for conducting the Yak-130's state acceptance trials. The first two machines were to be submitted for the state tests in May 2005. Plans in hand envisage the completion of the first stage of these tests in December 2005; their results will form the basis for a preliminary decision on putting the Yak-130 into series production. The entire programme of the state acceptance trials, including the spin test flights and live weapons trials, is to be completed in 2006, whereupon deliveries to Air Force units can begin.

At present the Russian Air Force has ordered four Yak-130s and an order for a further ten machines is being negotiated. As for later deliveries, the Air Force C-in-C quoted a figure of 200 to 300 machines. Although the number of Yak-130s to be ordered by the Air Force has not been finalised, a contract has been signed with the Sokol aircraft plant for the manufacture of an initial batch of 12 aircraft in 2005-07; production can start after Stage A of the state acceptance trials has been completed and the so-called preliminary conclusion issued. The first machine of the initial batch could then be delivered in mid-2006, with the delivery of the 12th aircraft taking place in late 2007. Subsequently the Sokol plant would be able to make deliveries of production aircraft at the rate of some 12 machines per year.

The Russian Air Force plans to buy the Yak-130 in order to replace the Czech-built Aero L-39C Albatros trainers which currently form the backbone of its training fleet.

The prospect of the Yak-130's introduction into the Russian Air Force inventory led the Yakovlev OKB to step up the efforts to promote the aircraft also to the world market. By mid-2004 the Rosoboronexport State Company handling Russian arms exports had held technical demonstrations of the Yak-130 in Algeria, India, Germany, the Ukraine, Chile and Slovakia, as well as Malaysia, Indonesia, Thailand and a number of African countries. The Yakovlev Design Bureau has reached an agreement with the Sukhoi Holding Company under the terms of which the sale of Sukhoi aircraft will be accompanied by an offer of the Yak-130 as a training aircraft within a package deal. Yakovlev hopes to occupy up to thirty per cent of the world trainer/combat trainer market.

The Yak-130 has growth potential that enables the development of its various versions. Plans are in hand to develop a shipboard trainer, a light single-seat fighter, a light attack aircraft, a light reconnaissance plane (operating jointly with the Pchela UAV) and an unmanned attack aircraft.

Above: The second production-standard Yak-130 after being painted in the same colour scheme as the first aircraft and becoming '02 White'.

In an effort to boost the export potential of the Yak/AEM-130, the Yakovlev OKB and Aermacchi studied the possibility of re-engining the aircraft with F124 turbofans developed by the International Turbine Engine Co. (ITEC, a subsidiary of the AlliedSignal company) and derated to 25 kN. The dissolution of the partnership between Yakovlev and Aermacchi put an end to these joint studies, but the F124 engine was, in fact, chosen by the Italian company for its own version of the Yak-130 (see below).

As mentioned above, in December 1999 Yakovlev and Aermacchi went their separate ways in the further development of the basic design. Aermacchi reportedly received a full set of documentation on the Yak-130 from the Russian side in accordance with an agreement between the governments of Russia and Italy; the transfer of documentation was

Russian Air Force C-in-C Vladimir Mikhailov (right) shakes the hand of Yakovlev chief test pilot Roman Taskayev after a ride in the Yak-130.

Above: Yak-130 '02 White' climbs away as the main gear doors close. Note the weapons pylons under the wings.
Below: The same aircraft on final approach. No pylons are fitted this time. Note the pitot heads under the nose and at the tip pf the radome.

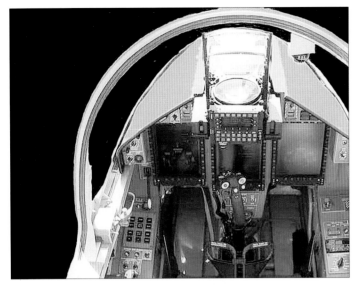 

Both cockpits of the production-standard aircraft (the front cockpit featuring a head-up display is on the left) feature three 6x8 inch colour MFDs and an I/O panel above them. In the lower row of pictures, the MFDs show, left to right: the primary flight instruments, the tactical situation and systems status.

regarded as a part payment of the Russian debt to Italy.

On the basis of this documentation the Italian company reworked the design to suit the requirements of prospective Western customers and produced its own 'Westernised' version of the Yak-130 which received the designation Aermacchi M-346. Externally this lead-in fighter trainer is very similar to the first Yak-130 prototype, but it features a complete structural redesign, a Western set of avionics and Western engines – the aircraft is powered by two Honeywell/FIAT Avio F124-200 turbofans developed jointly by engine manufacturers of the US and Italy. Aermacchi is positioning the aircraft to meet the 12-nation AJEPT (Advanced European Jet Pilot Training) 'Eurotraining' requirement.

Coded P.01, the first prototype (c/n 6962) was completed on 7th June 2003. It was described as an advanced and lead-in fighter trainer. The first flight took place on 15th July 2004. When presenting the M-346, Aermacchi accentuated such features as vortex aerodynamics, the digital FBW control system per-

mitting a controlled flight at AoAs up to 40°, modular avionics, 'glass' cockpits and so on. The aircraft is powered by two F124-200s which ensure a thrust/weight ratio close to 1.

Under the terms of the Yakovlev/Aermacchi agreement, Aermacchi has the exclusive

right to market its trainer in NATO member-countries, while Yakovlev has the exclusive right to the CIS market. In other parts of the world the two companies will engage in free market competition, leaving it up to the customers to decide which aircraft they want.

Specifications of the Yak-130 combat trainer

	Yak-130D	Production Yak-130
Engine type	DV-2	AI-222-25
Engine thrust at take-off, kgp (lbst)	2,200 (4,850)	2,500 kg (5,512)
Length	11.245 m (36 ft 10¾ in)	n.a.
Wing span	10.4 m (34 ft 1½ in)	n.a.
Wing area, m² (sq ft)	23.5 (253)	n.a.
Empty weight, equipped, kg (lb)	4,410 (9,720)	n.a.
All-up weight, kg (lb)	6,200 (13,670) clean	
	9,000 (19,840) maximum	c. 9,000 (19,850)
Maximum speed, km/h (mph)	1,050 (652)	1,060 (659)
Landing speed, km/h (mph)	175 (109)	n.a.
Service ceiling, m (ft)	12,500 (41,000)	12,000 (39,360)
Range, km (miles)	2,220 (1,379)	2,000 (1,240)
Landing run, m (ft)	485 (1,590)	n.a.

Above: The cockpit section of Yak-130 '02 Black'. The Yak-130 is the first Russian military aircraft to feature a micro detonating cord (MDC) for shattering the cockpit canopy before ejection.

Above: A dummy KAB-500T bomb and a B-13L FFAR pod under the port wing of Yak-130 '02 White' in the static park of the MAKS-2005 airshow. '01 White' was in the flying display.

The handsomely painted Aermacchi M-346 prototype at the 2005 Paris Air Show. The similarity to the Yak-130 is obvious.

Yak-130 – Various Project Versions

The use of the Yak-130 in a light fighter role was one of the options considered by the Yakovlev OKB. No details are available as of this writing.

The prospective versions of the Yak-130 include a shipboard trainer meant to replace the Su-25UTG in the Russian Navy, as well as for export.

The project versions of the Yak-130 also include a four-seat (!) trainer version featuring a wider forward fuselage with two side-by-side pairs of seats in tandem. It is intended for training pilots and navigators of military transport aircraft and bombers, as well as airline pilots.

A shipboard (carrier on-board delivery) version of the four-seat Yak-130 derivative is intended for quick delivery of people and small cargoes to aircraft carriers. This aircraft is expected to have a maximum cruising speed of 650 km/h (404 mph) and a practical range of 2,000 km (1,243 miles).

Yak-131 Single-Seat Light Strike Aircraft (Project)

A report published in mid-2003 stated that there were plans envisaging the development of a dedicated strike derivative of the Yak-130. This machine designated Yak-131 will be a lightweight single-seat aircraft possessing 90 to 95% commonality with the basic Yak-130. The strike version will have its combat radius extended to 1,000 km (620 miles). It will be provided with a built-in 30-mm cannon. The weapon complement will also include the Vikhr' (Whirlwind) laser-guided anti-tank missiles.

The light strike aircraft version of the Yak-130 will feature armour protection making use of lightweight composite materials; this will afford grater survivability. A new avionics suite will enable the aircraft to tackle its combat tasks day and night under adverse weather conditions. It is to be equipped with the Moskit-2 radar (an improved version of the earlier Moskit radar developed by NPO Fazotron). The Yak-131 was visualised as part of a unified reconnaissance/strike system comprising also a reconnaissance/target designator aircraft, as well as unmanned reconnaissance drones. The Yak-131 was expected to carry up to 3,000 kg (6,615 lb) of armament externally on nine weapons pylons. External stores options comprised up to eight free-fall bombs weighing up to 250 kg (551 lb) each, up to four guided bombs weighing up to 500 kg (1,102 lb) each, the Kh-25ML air-to-surface missile or (on export versions) the AGM-65 Maverick missile, as well as short- or medium-range air-to-air missiles.

Yak-135 Supersonic Derivative

A brief mention was made in press reports of the possibility of the Yak-130 being developed into a supersonic light strike and multipurpose aircraft designated Yak-135.

Chapter 4

Upgrading the Strategic Aircraft

The nearest future of the Russian strategic bomber arm (DA – **Dahl'nyaya avi***a*htsiya, Long-Range Aviation) is associated with the upgrading of the aircraft it now operates – primarily the Tu-95MS and Tu-160 strategic missile-carriers. As a rule, the 'age' of most aircraft currently operated by the Long-Range Aviation does not exceed 10-15 years; thus, their remaining designated service life allows them to soldier on at least until 2015. However, if one takes into account the example of the Tu-16 and Tu-95 dating back to the mid/late 1950s (these bombers remained in service for nearly 40 years), the current aircraft may remain in service well beyond 2015. The upgrading will be concerned mainly with the avionics and equipment of the missile carrier aircraft and will envisage supplementing their arsenal with new types of weapons – in particular, new medium-range and long-range cruise missiles with conventional warheads (such as the Kh-555).

Such new weapons, in their non-nuclear versions, were developed a few years ago and are in the middle of their test programme. The Air Force Command evolved a programme for adding them to the weapons range of the Tu-95MS and Tu-160. The implementation of the programme was based on the assumption that the necessary state funds would be allocated. In parallel with the upgrading, work was to be effected on extending the aircraft's designated service life and actual life span.

On 26th May 2005 the Russian Academy of Sciences held a 'round table' conference on innovations in the defence industry. Speaking at this forum, Lieutenant-General Aleksandr Rakhmanov, Deputy Chief of the Armaments Board of the Russian Armed Forces, declared that a precision-guided long-range cruise missile had been developed and successfully tested in Russia; this cruise missile is to be carried by Tu-95MS and Tu-160 strategic missile carriers operated by the 37th Strategic Air Army of the Supreme Command (that is, the DA) and currently undergoing an upgrade. 'Recently a demonstration was held of our precision-guided air-launched missile. Launched from a distance of two thousand kilometres [1,240 miles], it flew right into the window, as they say in aviation', said Rakhmanov.

Experts believe that the Kh-555 missile which the general was referring to has been developed as a derivative of the production Kh-55MS which has up to now been the principal armament of the Tu-160 and Tu-95MS. Apparently the Kh-555 differs from its precursor in having a conventional warhead, as well as in being equipped with optical (TV) homing equipment as a part of its guidance system. Deliveries of such missiles to the DA, which currently operates a fleet of some fifteen Tu-160s and some sixty Tu-95MS missile carriers, began in 2004.

A few years ago Russian Air Force Commander-in-Chief Army General Vladimir Mikhailov paid a visit to the Kazan' Aircraft

Above: A stripped-down Tu-95MS undergoing refurbishment at the Russian Air Force's ARZ No.360 at Dyaghilevo AB near Ryazan'.

Tu-95MS *Bear-H* missile carriers, like this somewhat incomplete example awaiting overhaul, are due to have new weapons integrated.

Above: Some of the Tu-95MSs now in service with the Russian Air Force's 37th Strategic Air Army are named after Russian cities. This one, '12 Red', is christened *Moskva* (Moscow) and bears the city crest with St. George And The Dragon, as well as the Gold Star Order reflecting Moscow's Heroic City status.

Above: Tu-95MS '19 Red' stages through a transport aviation base en route to the High North for an exercise, taxying past a row of resident quasi-civil Ilyushin IL-76MD transports. It wears 13 mission markers aft of the flightdeck.

Tu-95MS '23 Red' is named *Tambov* after a city in central Russia. Coloured propeller spinner tips are often encountered on Soviet/CIS military turboprop aircraft.

Above: Though many may dismiss turboprops as outdated, the Tu-95MS still offers impressive capabilities. It also looks impressive – a graceful aircraft (not to mention the sound, that distinctive throbbing roar of the four contra-rotating propellers which is sweet music to any aviation enthusiast's ears).

The DA's other principal type of today is the swing-wing Tu-160, and most examples are named after notable persons – not necessarily airmen. '07 Red' seen here making a high-speed pass with the wings at maximum sweep is named after Aleksandr Molodchiy (twice Hero of the Soviet Union), a wartime bomber pilot.

Left: Tu-160 '12 Red' is named after Aleksandr Novikov, an Air Chief Marshal of the 1940s.

Below left: Tu-160 '11 Red' honours Vasiliy Sen'ko, the only bomber navigator to become twice Hero of the Soviet Union during the Great Patriotic War.

Above: An interesting formation of two Russian Air Force swing-wing bomber types – the Su-24M and the Tu-22M3.

Right: Face to face with the Tu-22M3.

Production Association named after Sergey P. Gorbunov (KAPO) which manufactures the Tu-160. The visit resulted in the signing of a Letter of Intent in the field of aircraft construction with the Government of the Republic of Tatarstan. Among other things, it confirmed the Russian Air Force's intention to place a state order for the refurbishment and upgrading of the Tu-160 strategic bombers at KAPO.

The Tupolev Joint-Stock Co. prepared several upgrade options for the Tu-160 differing in the scope of modifications which, in turn, depended on the funding available. The main content of the upgrade was concerned with perfecting the avionics suite and the armament of the bomber by providing it with new PGMs.

The Ministry of Defence signed an agreement with KAPO on the repairs and modernisation of all Tu-160s currently on strength with the Russian Air Force so that they will be able to remain in service at least until 2030. Such a

Above: A Tu-22M3 undergoing refurbishment at ARZ No.360; the huge radome and revolving antenna of the PNA-D radar have been removed. This type is also due for a mid-life update.

lengthy period is due to the fact that deliveries of production Tu-160s to the DA's first-line units began as late as 1987, and the 'youngest' Tu-160 was built by KAPO in 2000.

Recently two Tu-160s were being kept at the Kazan' aircraft plant. One of them was taken directly from a first-line bomber regiment at Engels-2 AB, while the other had been a 'dogship' used by the Tupolev JSC in test programmes. After the completion of repairs and upgrading both machines are scheduled to go to Engels. This will restore the Russian Air Force's Tu-160 fleet to its previous level of 15 machines, making up for the tragic loss of one aircraft in a fatal accident in September 2003. In late December 2004, during the festivities on occasion of the Russian Long-Range Aviation's 90th anniversary,

Lieutenant-General Igor' Khvorov, Commander of the 37th Strategic Air Army of the Supreme Command, said: 'Soon we shall take delivery of two new Tu-160 aircraft from the Kazan' plant. One of them will feature so radical an upgrade that it will retain only the outward shape of its previous self. This will be a modern bomber fitted with a state-of-the-art onboard digital computer which will entail a complete change of the weapon system bringing it to a higher order of magnitude in comparison with those currently in use'. The General was referring, in particular, to the new digital computer enabling the bomber to make the fullest use of satellite navigation.

Thus, with the service introduction of medium- and long-range air-launched precision-guided cruise missiles the Russian Long-Range Aviation acquires a new quality which will enhance its role in ensuring the military security of Russia in the case of any contingency in world affairs. The Long-Range Aviation will be endowed with a unique capability of theatre and strategic significance: it will be simultaneously a real strategic means of both nuclear and non-nuclear deterrence.

The Tu-22M3 bombers still remaining in service will be next to undergo an upgrade. For example, one of the upgrade variants is proposed by the Gefest & T JSC, an avionics and armament integration company which had previously developed a successful upgrade option for the Su-24M (see Chapter One). Plans in hand also envisage equipping the

This operational Tu-22M3 from Shaykovka AB paid a brief visit to Zhukovskiy in August 2005 in order to participate in a formation flypast of Tupolev aircraft at the MAKS-2005 airshow.

Tu-22M3s with the SVP-24 specialised computing subsystem and with an 'electronic geographical map'. This will enhance the aircraft's combat potential considerably. The Tu-22M3 will acquire the capability to approach the target at ultra-low altitude and deliver a strike with utmost precision. At present Gefest & T is engaged in developing the means of attack that will be used against targets of theatre importance (that is, situated far behind the frontline) from a corresponding point on the aircraft's route. This task is very topical, among other things, because it affords effective means of combating terrorists who, as we know, do not give prior warning of their actions. The new equipment will deprive them of the possibility to make unexpected manoeuvres.

As for the requirements that will come on the agenda in a more distant future, they will be met by a radically new type of long-range missile strike aircraft. Preliminary work on the Future Long-Range Aviation Airborne System (PAK DA – *Perspektivnyy aviatsionnyy kompleks Dahl'ney aviahtsii*) programme has been in progress for several years now; according to statements made by the Russian Air Force C-in-C, the prototype of such an aircraft can be built and submitted for testing approximately in the middle of the 21st century's second decade.

Assessing the current state of Russia's Long-Range Aviation, we may justly conclude that, despite a considerable reduction in the number of aircraft on strength, it retains quite impressive combat capabilities. These will be further enhanced to meet the challenges of the time after the implementation of upgrade programmes and introduction of new air-to-surface weapons types.

IL-38N and IL-38SD ASW/Maritime Patrol Aircraft

One of the most notable events of the second International Maritime Defence Show (IMDS-2005) held in St. Petersburg between 29th June and 3rd July 2005 was the presentation of a maritime targeting/observation systems family for aircraft and helicopters of various classes and types, performed by an institute forming part of the Leninets Holding Co.

Testing of the first upgraded Ilyushin IL-38N anti-submarine warfare aircraft has been under way since 2001; the N refers to the *Novella* (Novel) new-generation avionics suite with which it is equipped. Plans in hand envisage the completion of state acceptance trials and delivery of the first upgraded ASW system to the Russian Navy in 2005; subsequently, using this first aircraft as a pattern, the entire IL-38 fleet of the Russian Naval Aviation is to be upgraded to IL-38N standard at the MoD's Aircraft Repair Plant No.20 (ARZ No.20) in Pushkin near St. Petersburg.

Above: '19 Red', the prototype of the IL-38N upgrade. The flattened housing carried on struts above the forward fuselage – the most obvious recognition feature of the IL-38N – houses ELINT equipment; the ventral radome appears unchanged but in fact houses a new radar.

By the summer of 2005 a similar upgrade had already been effected on three Indian Navy IL-38s. These are equipped with the export version of the Novella system known as Morskoy Zmey (Sea Dragon), hence the different designation IL-38SD. Visitors examining the aircraft displayed statically at Pushkin airfield as part of the IMDS-2005 could see for themselves that these systems had actually been incorporated into patrol and ASW aircraft. One of the Russian IL-38Ns, under test at present, and an example of the Indian IL-38SD could be seen at Pushkin.

According to the information distributed at the show by the manufacturer, the Sea Dragon system comprises a wide range of information and search systems (radar, ELINT package, thermal imaging, magnetic anomaly detection and sonar systems, a dunking sonar module), two standardised operator work stations equipped with modern display systems and dispersed computing environment with a multi-level processing of information and automation of the processes of detecting the targets, transmitting information about them and destroying the targets.

Above: Another view of IL-38N '19 Red' at Pushkin.

In June-July 2005 the IL-38N was on display at Pushkin as part of the International Maritime Defence Show.

Above: Close-up of the IL-38N at Pushkin, with an Indian Navy IL-38SD serialled IN303 visible beyond. Note the small 'ball turret' of the gyrostabilised thermal imaging system under the IL-38N's extreme nose.

The Sea Dragon system includes a search radar with a slotted antenna array which, in the case of the IL-38, is accommodated in the existing quasi-spherical radome under the front fuselage formerly occupied by the *Berkoot* (Golden Eagle) radar. The radar is able to detect maritime surface targets at distances up to the radio-wave horizon, and aerial targets at distances up to 350 km (218 miles). The thermal imaging system (its 'ball' stabilised about the three axes and provided with five optical windows is located in the extreme nose of the IL-38) is capable of detecting, tracking and identifying surface targets with high precision and of performing automatic tracking using target designation from the radar. The ELINT system gives 360° coverage (on the IL-38 aircraft it is accommodated in a flattened boxy container mounted on special struts above the forward fuselage just aft of the flightdeck); the shape of these struts is different on the IL-38N and the

The IL-38N on final approach to Pushkin.

Above: The Indian Navy's IL-38SD has the ELINT array mounted on three short pylons instead of the Russian IL-38N's lattice-like structure, and the shape of the fairing and the blade aerial on top of it are also different.

Another aspect of IL-38SD IN303 gleaming with fresh paint after the overhaul which coincided with the upgrade. The Indian Navy titles are in English to port and in Bengali to starboard; the DAB tailcode denotes Indian Navy Air Station Dabolim located in the country's smallest state, Goa.

Above: The number 301 on the nose reveals that this unpainted IL-38 seen during an early post-overhaul checkout flight is an Indian Navy machine (IN301). The aircraft is presumably also due for conversion into an IL-38SD. The upgrade is a very welcome enhancement of the Indian Navy's capabilities, considering that two of its IL-38s were lost in a tragic and absurd mid-air collision over Goa on 1st October 2002.

IL-38SD (the latter has three airfoil-section struts instead of a plethora of V-struts). It can reconnoitre radiation-emitting targets within a broad range of frequencies (6.5-40 GHz), determining the parameters of the electromagnetic pulses intercepted and comparing it to the available 'identification library' which contains up to 2,000 types of electronic systems. The magnetic anomaly detector (on the IL-38 it is accommodated in the usual 'sting' fairing located aft of the tail unit) detects magnetic anomalies at distances up to 900 m (2,950 ft). The sonobuoy system detects submarines by the noise they produce, making use of a set of RGB-47E and RGB-41E passive omnidirectional and directional sonobuoys, as well as GB-58E active sonobuoys and RTB-93E radio sonobuoys. Each of the two operator workstations is provided with two colour multi-function displays measuring 15 inches diagonally and a sensor control panel.

One more view of IN301 landing at Pushkin. The black nose cap is dielectric.

Chapter 5

Militant Mils

Mi-24PN Combat Helicopter

The Russian Mil' Mi-24 combat helicopter is well known all over the world. It has been operated by more than 30 nations. The years that have passed and the events in which this helicopter has taken part, and is taking part to this day, have corroborated its high performance and its ability to make itself indispensable in the conduct of military operations. No sooner was the Mi-24 introduced into service that it became a participant of actual warfare virtually on all territories making up the Soviet Union's area of strategic interests. The helicopter took part in numerous armed conflicts, but the Afghan War proved to be the greatest and hardest test for it.

Gradually, as the helicopter was fully mastered in service and combat experience with the type was accumulated, the range of missions for which the Mi-24 was suitable became more clearly defined. These included,

first and foremost, the support of ground forces during offensive and defensive operations; escorting tactical assault groups delivered by transport helicopters and providing fire support for them; transporting reconnaissance and *spetsnaz* (commando) groups. Later the range of missions accomplished by the Mi-24 was supplemented by one more task – escorting transport aircraft at the moment of their take-off and landing in the vicinity of combat areas.

What, then, is the reason for the Mi-24 being so popular as a combat helicopter? After all, to this day it remains in service with several NATO nations which had previously been part of the Eastern Bloc.

First of all, it is survivability. The Mi-24 has efficient armour protection: armour plate 4-5 mm (0⁵⁄₃₂ to 0³⁄₁₆ in) thick shields the vital components (engine accessory gearboxes,

engine oil tanks, the main gearbox, the hydraulic tank). When the helicopter comes under heavy machine-gun (HMG) fire, it is the powerplant that takes punishment most often. But the Mi-24 can make it back to base even with only one engine operative, running in the contingency mode. If pierced by an HMG bullet, the main gearbox is capable of functioning for some 15-20 minutes despite losing oil. Designers of the Mi-24 have succeeded in providing the machine with ingeniously arranged back-up systems which make it possible to bring the machine home even with the hydraulics and electric power supply systems damaged. Analysis of the helicopter's combat losses has revealed that the well-protected crew is capable of bringing the machine safely back to base.

The experience gained in the course of the Mi-24's involvement in actual combat has

'11 White', the Mi-24PN demonstrator in black airshow colours with white/yellow trim and the Mil' logo. This view shows the fixed landing gear (note the absence of the dished main gear doors), the clipped wings and the 'proboscis' carrying the Zarevo opto-electronic targeting system.

Above: Another view of Mi-24PN '11 White' at Torzhok. The standard three-bladed tail rotor is retained in this instance, as is the Raduga-Sh missile guidance system under the nose.

Here the Mi-24PN prototype is seen with ferry tanks on the inboard pylons. Note the colour of the optical coating on the faceted sensor window of the Zarevo system. The orifice below the rear (pilot's) cockpit is a landing light with an infra-red filter for use with night vision goggles.

Above: Despite the clipped wings, the Mi-24PN can carry more anti-tank guided missiles than the standard Mi-24P thanks to the racks (as seen here) for extremely neat eight-packs of 9M120 Ataka ATGM.

Mi-24PN '11 White' takes off on a test flight.

Above: Mi-24PN '11 White' is seen here carrying four 20-round B-8V20 rocket pods. Even the overall black finish cannot disguise the soot deposits from the engines.

Above: The pilot's cockpit of the Mi-24PN features a single colour MFD.

Close-up of the Zarevo opto-electronic targeting system designed by the Krasnogorsk Optomechanical Plant (KOMZ), with a van reflected in the sensor window. The inscription says 'Danger, laser radiation'.

been thoroughly analysed; as a result, a combat survivability enhancement programme for the helicopter has been evolved and progressively put into effect. For example, the passive protection means (armour plating of the crew cockpits and vital systems) were supplemented by means of protection against guided weapons. From 1980 onwards the engine exhausts of the helicopter are provided with air/exhaust mixers to protect the helicopter from shoulder-launched SAMs. Initially the Mi-24s were provided with two ASO-2V dispensers, each housing 32 decoy flares; in 1978 this arrangement gave place to two angled units, each comprising three dispensers, scabbed onto the fuselage sides. These create a wide trail made up of decoy flares. From 1982 onwards the helicopter's system of self-protection is supplemented by the Lipa active IRCM jammer. In the early-production Mi-24A and Mi-24D helicopters up to 90% of the total battle damage was inflicted on the fuel tanks. In the subsequent versions the fuel tanks were provided with a self-sealing liner and filled with polyurethane foam which considerably lessened the risk involved in getting that sort of damage, preventing the helicopter from catching fire when hit.

The Mi-24's adjustment to different areas of its employment and climatic zones was effected directly in operational service, in combat. Under the 'hot and high' conditions vertical take-off was virtually never used and the crews practised only rolling take-offs. In consequence, proceeding from the need to raise the take-off weight, a take-off mode was developed in which the helicopter made a rolling take-off, resting on its nosewheels while the mainwheels were lifted off the runway. It was the Design Bureau's founder, Mikhail L. Mil', who suggested this method. The procedure was as follows: the machine took up a nose-down attitude with an inclination of 10-12° and performed a swift acceleration in ground effect. This technique made it possible to increase the take-off weight by 500-1,500 kg (1,102-3,306 lb), depending on the altitude of the helicopter airstrip.

The vast operational experience gained with the Mi-24 helicopters made it possible to polish the tactics of their combat use to perfection: the main emphasis was made on the element of surprise, the continuity of fire and mutual support. The main tactical operational procedure used in combat by the Mi-24 in Afghanistan (especially at the beginning of the war) was the fulfilment of combat missions at low altitude (up to 50 m/160 ft). However, the advent of the shoulder-launched SAMs compelled the helicopter crews to raise the altitude to 1,000 m (3,280 ft), and acquisition of large-calibre firearms by the enemy drove the Mi-24s to altitudes in excess of 1,500 m (4,920 ft).

The wars in Chechnya posed crews new, more complex tasks for the Mi-24 crews because the rebels now made use of a well-organised anti-aircraft defence system. In these conditions it was the crews of the Mi-24 helicopters that were tasked with destroying the shoulder-launched SAM systems immediately after the missile had been detected thanks to the distinctive smoke trail from the launch site. In Chechnya the Mi-24 helicopters flew strike sorties, escorted troop convoys and performed aerial reconnaissance. Attacks against ground targets were performed with high efficiency from altitudes of 3,000-2,500 m (9,840-8,200 ft) at flight path gradients of 10° to 25° and speeds of 140-150 km/h (87-93 mph).

In the years that have passed the Mi-24 helicopter has proved its worth as a reliable combat machine; moreover, operational practice has revealed the existence of substantial reserves for extending its life cycle. A joint effort of the Mil' Design Bureau and the production plants resulted in the creation of the most successful Mi-24V and Mi-24P versions; recently, in response to military requirements, these have been supplemented by a new version – the Mi-24PN which is capable of tackling not only the same missions as its predecessors, but also new, more complicated tasks. In accordance with a government programme adopted some years ago the work on upgrading the Mi-24 and Mi-8 helicopters for the benefit of the Ministry of Defence was given a high degree of priority.

The Mi-24PN (*pushechnyy, nochnoy* – cannon-armed, night-capable) is a 'night' version of the baseline Mi-24P modified for round-the-clock operations. Combat experience gained in the North Caucasian Theatre has proved the need for putting helicopters into action at night and in adverse weather.

Externally the Mi-24PN differs little from the baseline machine. The undercarriage legs are shortened and made non-retractable, a short 'proboscis' carrying a targeting system sensor turret is fitted ahead of the front cockpit. The most important changes are to be found inside. The helicopter is fitted with an avionics suite which enables it to tackle combat missions during night-time.

In response to requirements posed by the military the upgraded Mi-24PN was fitted with on-board equipment comprising:
• the *Raduga-Sh* (Rainbow-Sh) surveillance and aiming system integrated with the *Zarevo* (Glow) thermal imager developed by the Krasnogorsk Optomechanical Plant (KOMZ) named after Zverev;
• a laser rangefinder;
• a channel for guiding the 9M120 Ataka or 9M114 Shtoorm ATGMs.

The helicopter's integrated avionics suite incorporates liquid-crystal multi-function

Above: The nose of an operational Mi-24PN coded '36 Yellow' (c/n 26731).

Above: Another view of the same helicopter in the static park of the MAKS-2005 airshow. A protective cover closes the window of the Zarevo targeting system.

Close-up of the Mi-24PN prototype's fixed main gear units.

Above: An eight-pack of 9M120 Ataka ATGMs and a B-8V20 FFAR pod under the starboard wing of Mi-24PN '11 White'.

Above: A KMGU submunitions dispenser (used for mine-laying and the like) and a twin pack of 9M39 Igla-V air-to-air missiles for self-defence on Mi-24PN '11 White'.

displays (MFDs) and night-vision goggles coupled with the suitably adapted cockpit lighting equipment. To ensure night landings, the helicopter is provided with a special infra-red searchlight. The new avionics suite enables the Mi-24PN to fly combat missions around the clock with all the standard weapon systems and to be piloted safely at night at altitudes between 50 and 200 m (164-660 ft). A high degree of navigation accuracy is achieved thanks to the incorporation of a digital map coupled with the updating of co-ordinates through the satellite navigation system. In addition to working with both of today's principal systems – the Western NAVSTAR and the Russian GLONASS, – the satellite navigation equipment can also operate in a joint mode, making use of the information supplied simultaneously by the satellites of both systems. This is the first satellite navigation system adopted as standard for service use in military helicopter aviation.

Night flights at extremely low altitudes require tremendous concentration on the part of the pilot. Naturally, any attempt to measure the pilot workload in figures and percentages is highly arbitrary and approximate, but one can safely assume that up to 85% of attention is devoted to the monitoring and surveillance of the space outside the cockpit and only 15% remains available for watching the readings of the instruments. The additional flight and navigation equipment fitted to the upgraded Mi-24PN, as listed above, considerably reduces the workload of the pilot and the weapons systems operator by presenting the necessary flight information in concentrated form. For the first time on a Russian helicopter, data is presented with the help of independently functioning colour MFDs installed both in the pilot's cockpit and at the WSO's workstation. The MFD can operate in primary flight display mode, duplicating the readings of standard electromechanical

A quartet of operational Mi-24PNs equipped with long-range tanks and FFAR pods prepares to redeploy to another airfield, probably for an exercise.

Above and below: Mi-24PN '29 Yellow', one of several operated by the 344th Combat & Conversion Training Centre in Torzhok, at its home base with the starboard troop cabin door open. The helicopter is fairly weathered, except for the cockpit section which is usually wrapped in tarpaulins when on the ground.

Above: Mi-24PNs '28 Yellow' and '29 Yellow' at the Flying Legends-2005 air fest at Monino airfield near Moscow on 29th July 2005.
Below: All four 344th TsBP i PLS Mi-24PNs present at Flying Legends-2005 make a flypast in echelon starboard formation.

Above and below: Gleaming with fresh paint, Mi-24PN '37 Yellow' performs at Monino. Three of the four choppers seen at the event appeared to be freshly overhauled and upgraded.

Above and below: Mi-24PN '58 Red' put on a solo display at Monino.
Right: '58 Red' and '29 Yellow' make a formation flypast. The colour and style of the tactical codes on the 344th Centre's helicopters varies widely.

instruments. The navigation section of the display presents a map which carries a superimposed basic outline of the route; it is possible to change the scale of the image and alter its orientation (adjusting it to the direction of flight or to the traditional orientation with 'North at the top'). The MFD also shows the picture from the thermal imager plus aiming reticles and target range as supplied by the laser rangefinder. This information is especially important when using unguided rockets because it makes it possible to achieve higher accuracy. As we know, unguided rockets follow a ballistic trajectory, and the aiming reticles are issued with due account for corrections allowing for the wind direction which are determined by the computer.

As a whole, the avionics suite functions in semi-automatic mode; the WSO has only to identify and select the target, measure the distance with the help of the laser rangefinder, superimpose the moving mark on the target on the MFD and push the firing button. The avionics suite automatically computes a correction taking into account the distance, the flight speed and the wind speed; in calculating the correction the computer solves a three-dimensional ballistic task. Training in the operational use of the Mi-24PN conducted by pilots of the Russian Air Force's 344th Combat & Conversion Training Centre (TsBP i PLS) in Torzhok corroborated the effective-

ness of the computer's work. The new onboard flight and navigation avionics suite makes it possible to bring the machine to a pre-determined point on the route with a precision of up to 50-70 m (164-230 ft) in the automatic mode, following any one of five pre-programmed routes (taking account of waypoints).

The Mi-24PN is armed with the NPU-30 fixed cannon installation: a 30-mm (1.18 calibre) GSh-2-30 double-barrel cannon with a complement of 250 rounds. Weapons carried on the wing pylons can include up to sixteen 9M120 anti-tank guided missiles making up part of the Ataka-V system, or 9M120F or 9M114 Shtoorm ATGMs, up to ten S-13

The pilot of a Mi-24PN receives last-minute instructions from a ground crewman.

Above: Mi-24PN '29 Yellow' parked at Monino on 29th July, with private houses and a hangar belonging to the Central Russian Air Force Museum in the background.

'29 Yellow' was the first of the Mi-24PNs to land after the flying display, and after shutting down the crew took the opportunity to make a quick inspection of the engines. Note the vortex-type intake dust/debris filters removed to allow inspection of the engine compressor faces.

Above: Mi-24PN '36 Yellow' taxies at Zhukovskiy after arriving for the MAKS-2005 airshow. Again, the glossy paint is indicative of a recent overhaul.

unguided rockets, up to eighty S-8 unguided rockets, cannon pods with 23-mm (.90 calibre) cannons and 250 rounds each, and up to two air-to-air missiles. The effectiveness of the upgraded helicopter, in the opinion of military experts, exceeds that of the baseline Mi-24P by a factor of 1.5 to 1.7.

For the purpose of ferrying the helicopter over big distances, provision is made for the installation of new auxiliary fuel tanks identical to those of the Mi-28N helicopter. The fixed undercarriage does not mar the helicopter's aerodynamics too much because in combat missions flown at extremely low altitudes the helicopter flies at fairly low speeds – some 160 km/h (99 mph) – and the increase in drag and fuel consumption at such speeds does not exceed 1 or 2%. The night vision system makes it possible to detect targets at a distance of up to 3,500 m (11,480 ft). The new navigation/ attack avionics system has appreciably enhanced the helicopter's capabilities under the conditions of actual warfare, especially when it is necessary to achieve high accuracy in delivering unguided munitions.

As stated previously, the Mi-24PN was developed in response to requirements posed by the Russian military. In 2003 the first two Mi-24P helicopters were upgraded to Mi-24PN standard in accordance with the State Defence Order; later three more heli-

copters were upgraded by the Rostvertol enterprise in Rostov-on-Don, one of the two plants which built the type.

These first five upgraded helicopters were officially turned over by the production plant to the 344th TsBP i PLS in February 2004; the ceremony took place in Rostov-on-Don. The 344th TsBP i PLS started conversion training

of pilots selected for flying these machines. It is also known that a part of the service tests was conducted by Russian pilots in 2004 in Kyrghyzstan, when a Kamov Ka-50 attack helicopter and a Mi-24PN were deployed to Kant AB from Torzhok.

The Mi-24PN was publicly demonstrated by the Russian Air force during the Flying

The same machine in the static park of the MAKS-2005 airshow.

Legends-2005 airshow at Monino airfield near Moscow on 26th-29th July 2005 where four upgraded helicopters coded '28 Yellow', '29 Yellow', '37 Yellow' and '58 Red' performed group aerobatics. Just over two weeks later another upgraded machine from Torzhok ('36 Yellow', c/n 26731) was demonstrated in the static park of the MAKS-2005 airshow in Zhukovskiy (16th-21st August).

Importantly, the upgrading of Mi-24 helicopters to Mi-24PN standard can be effected not only at the production plant, but also by the Air Force's repair plants in the process of an overhaul accompanied by a service life extension. The main concept involves the so-called 'package upgrading' in accordance with which the Mi-24 helicopters can be upgraded into the Mi-24PN, Mi-24PK and Mi-35 versions (the latter for export). It is up to the customer to choose the upgrade variant.

Mi-28N Night Hunter Combat Helicopter

In the course of the last 30 years the Mi-24 has been the main attack helicopter of the Ground Forces of Russia, as well as of a number of countries in Eastern Europe, Asia and Latin America. The experience of the Mi-24's operational use in local wars and military conflicts, as well as its inherent potential for improvement, have made it possible to enhance its combat efficiency in the process of upgrading. However, when conducting intensive combat operations in the conditions of a strong enemy anti-aircraft defence, the Mi-24 had a number of substantial limitations. Therefore the task of creating a new-generation combat helicopter capable of destroying the enemy's armoured vehicles and fortifications, remained on the agenda.

Above: Head-on view of Mi-24PN '36 Yellow', showing the 'horns' of the Beryoza radar warning receiver antennas on the forward fuselage sides.

'31 Yellow', another 344th TsBP i PLS Mi-24PN, at a dispersal area in Torzhok.

Above: The first prototype Mi-28N in its current guise as '014 Yellow' with a spherical radome of the mast-mounted Arbalet radar; originally the machine was flown as '014 White outline' and had a cylindrical insert in the middle of the radome. Note the air data boom attached to the barrel of the 2A42 cannon for the duration of the tests.

The Mi-28 helicopter, and later its night-capable Mi-28N version dubbed 'Night Hunter', was intended to serve as a flying platform for carrying a weapons system and developed with due regard to the experience accumulated with the Mi-24 and other helicopters in the same class. The advanced development project of the Mi-28N was approved by the customer (the Russian Ministry of Defence) in 1993. The maiden flight of the prototype, originally coded '014 White outline', took place on 14th November 1996 with test pilot V. V. Yoodin and test navigator S. V. Nikulin at the controls. Manufacturer's tests began on 30th April 1997.

When developing the Mi-28N, its designers placed the main emphasis, among other things, on ensuring the simplicity of the helicopter's maintenance. For the first time in Soviet/Russian practice the design of the main rotor hub incorporated spherical elastomeric hinges instead of the drag, flapping and pitch hinges. In other hinges of the hub use was made of self-lubricating metal/teflon and textile bearings. As a result, the number of lubrication points was reduced to a minimum. The Mi-28N was fitted with a squashed-X tail rotor possessing higher performance and a lower noise signature.

The absence of a traditional cargo/troop cabin (albeit one or two persons can be accommodated in the radio equipment bay in case of need) made it possible to locate the heaviest units and systems close to the centre of gravity. As a result, the inertia forces were substantially reduced as compared to the Mi-24, especially along the longitudinal axis. The low position of the tailboom precluded the possibility of the main rotor blades striking it even during violent manoeuvres with high G forces.

The fuselage is designed in a fashion traditional for Mil' helicopters as an all-metal semi-monocoque structure of variable cross-section. It comprises the forward and centre

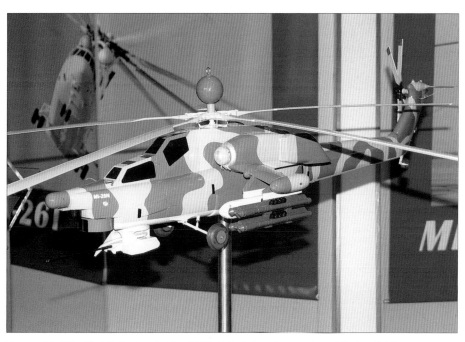

This model of the Mi-28N displayed at the MAKS-2005 airshow features four 9M39 Igla-V AAMs and a B-13L FFAR pod on the port wing pylons.

Above: This model of the Mi-28N, painted a rather shocking blue colour, was displayed at the 2005 Paris Air Show.

sections, the tailboom and the tail rotor pylon. The fuselage is made of aluminium alloys and composite materials making use of riveted and welded/bonded joints. Composite materials have also been used in the structures of the main and tail rotors, of the tail rotor pylon and in some units of secondary importance.

As distinct from the single-seat Ka-50, the helicopter has a traditional crew of two (a pilot and a WSO). The cockpits are pressurised and incorporate an air conditioning system. As on the Mi-24, the WSO sits ahead of and lower than the pilot. The forward fuselage houses avionics, targeting/observation systems and a flexible cannon mount. The cock-

pits feature all-round armour protection; the vital systems and units of the helicopter have multiple redundancy and are arranged in such a way that some units shield the others. Tests have shown that the sides of the fuselage can withstand hits from the US-produced General Electric M61A1 Vulcan 20-mm cannon.

Placed on the floor of the central fuselage is a self-sealing fuel tank container. Its upper panel accommodates electrical and radio equipment modules, as well as special equipment, which are arranged along the fuselage sides. An adjustable tailplane is mounted at the top of the tail rotor pylon. The helicopter is fitted with cantilever wings which are provided with four pylons for the carriage of weapons and auxiliary fuel tanks.

The powerplant of the Mi-28N comprises two TV3-117VMA turboshafts rated at 2,200 eshp apiece and an Ivchenko AI-9V auxiliary power unit. The engines have been developed by the Klimov Plant in St. Petersburg, which is the leading Russian enterprise in the field of helicopter engines. They represent one of the versions of the reliable TV3-117 engine family that has proved its worth in the course of many years of operation. The designers of the Mil' Moscow Helicopter Plant have plans for providing the helicopter with a

The second prototype Mi-28N, seen here at the Rostvertol factory's airfield in Rostov-on-Don in its original guise as '02 Yellow', had a spherical mast-mounted radome from the outset.

Above: As on the Mi-24, the cockpits are accessed from the opposite sides; the housings below the doors contain airbags which inflate if the doors are jettisoned so that the crewmembers do not strike the protruding elements of the airframe when bailing out.

much more advanced powerplant comprising two VK-2500 engines in due course. This will considerably enhance the helicopters' capabilities when operated in mountainous areas and in territories with a humid and hot climate.

To increase combat survivability, the engines of the Mi-28N are moved apart to the fuselage sides and separated from each other by the main gearbox, which reduces the prob-

ability of their being disabled by a single hit. In addition, the engine air intakes are provided with mushroom-like vortex-type dust filters, while the engine jetpipes are fitted with air/exhaust mixers reducing the helicopter's heat signature.

The TV3-117VMA is among the world's most reliable helicopter engines, proven in the course of many years of operation.

Should an engine failure nevertheless occur, thanks to a sufficient power reserve the Mi-28N is capable of continuing flight on one engine. The surviving engine automatically goes to contingency rating if the other engine cuts or is put out of action by enemy fire.

The fuel system of the Mi-28N has duplicated components for greater survivability, the fuel tanks are self-sealing and are filled

Another view of the pristine-looking second prototype at the factory airfield. The Mi-28 has a lean and predatory silhouette.

Above: A head-on view of '02 Yellow'. Two of the disposable launch tubes with 9M120 Ataka ATGMs are missing.

Mi-28N '02 Yellow' runs up its engines at Rostov-on-Don. Only eight of the 16 possible anti-tank guided missiles are fitted here; note the weathered appearance of the dorsal and nose radomes.

Above: The Mi-28N is rich in functional projections. The undernose turrets house low-light-level TV and laser ranging systems, the thimble radome on the nose is for the missile guidance antenna and the wingtip pods house ESM equipment. Note also the air data probe with a swivelling head.

Fitted with four auxiliary tanks, the second prototype Mi-28N is about to depart Rostov-on-Don on a ferry flight to Moscow. The strut on the starboard side of the nose appears to carry a video camera which is part of the test equipment.

Above: The second prototype Mi-28N hovers at Rostov-on-Don.

This view accentuates the long stroke of the levered-suspension main gear units and shows the lateral air intakes of the engines' exhaust/air mixers.

with polyurethane foam. The hydraulic system also has a back-up system.

The main rotor of the Mi-28N has five blades made of polymer composites, and the rotor hub has a titanium body with five spherical elastomeric hinges. The X-shaped four-blade tail rotor considerably reduces the noise level. The blades of the main and tail rotors are provided with a de-icing system.

The Mi-28N features a fixed tailwheel undercarriage. The main gear units and the crew seats are crashworthy. The main undercarriage legs incorporate oleo-pneumatic shock absorbers with extra travel for heavy landings. To enhance the safety of the crew in the case of an emergency landing with a high vertical speed, provision is made for a three-stage system for absorbing the kinetic energy after the impact against the ground:

• in a hard landing the undercarriage struts are deformed, thus converting a considerable portion of the impact energy into the deformation energy;

• part of the energy is absorbed by the crashworthy seats;

• a sinking floor absorbs the remaining impact energy.

The helicopter's life support system ensures crew safety during emergency landings with a vertical speed of up to 12 m/sec (39 ft/sec). In this case the G forces are reduced to a physiologically admissible level.

Introduction of new technical features has led to a considerable reduction of the volume of work necessary for the maintenance of the rotor system. This makes it possible to ensure maintenance of the machine during off-base operations (if the helicopter has to operate from ad hoc helipads). The design of the cannon installation makes it possible to partially disassemble the cannon without removing it.

The helicopter is fitted with an integrated avionics system (developed by the Ramenskoye-based RPKB company) which ensures the tackling of flight, navigation and targeting tasks day and night, in visual and instrument meteorological conditions. This includes nap-of-the-earth flying (that is, flight at 10-25 m (33-82 ft) with terrain following and obstacle avoidance). In this case use is made of digital map information and of a synthesised three-dimensional image of the locality. The system makes it possible:

• to detect and identify targets securely at any time of day or night;

• to make use of guided and unguided onboard weapons;

• to exercise control of groups of helicopters with an automated distribution of targets between them;

• to conduct automated exchange of target information between groups of helicopters, as well as with ground-based or airborne command posts.

Above: Here the drum-shaped thermal imager/laser ranger turret is rotated back to front, hiding the window from view; conversely, the windows of the smaller TV system turret are exposed.

Both cockpits have bulletproof windows all around and armour-plated walls and floors.

Above: The radome of the mast-mounted Arbalet radar.

Above left: The Mi-28 features permanently installed exhaust/air mixers directing the exhaust flow downward. Note the cowling and exhaust of the AI-9V APU aft of the main rotor hub and the formation lights on the wings.

Left: The 2A42 selectable-feed cannon with its two ammunition boxes for HE/fragmentation and armour-piercing ammunition.

Below and below left: Two more views of the cannon installation.

In addition, the onboard avionics suite monitors the functioning of the powerplant, power train, fuel system, hydraulics and pneumatic system, provides audio warning for the crew about emergency situations and ensures telephone communication between the crew and the ground personnel in the process of pre-flight preparations (external and internal radio communications are recorded). The avionics suite comprises:

• a stabilised targeting/observation unit in the WSO's cockpit with optical, thermal and TV channels of observation;

• a thermal imaging unit for the pilot and a laser range-finder;

• a helmet-mounted target acquisition and indication system;

• the pilot's night-vision goggles;

• an electronic flight instrumentation system with liquid-crystal colour MFDs;

• inertial and satellite navigation systems;

• navigation systems based on the use of Earth's physical fields;

• a communication suite;

• an *Arbalet* (Crossbow) mast-mounted multi-mode radar with a 360° field of view.

The multi-mode radar housed in a spherical radome mounted on top of the rotor mast enables the helicopter to detect targets while hiding behind natural objects and terrain features; in addition, the radar provides information about obstacles, including separate single trees and high-voltage power lines. It enables the helicopter to fly around the clock at extremely low altitudes even in adverse weather conditions; that is, it ensures the tackling not only of combat tasks, but of the flight and navigation tasks as well. The night-vision goggles provided for the crew serve the same purpose.

The helicopter features a system of map information with a high resolution and a data base on the terrain features in the combat area. Proceeding from these data, a computing system can form a three-dimensional image of the locality where the helicopter is flying. All this information is presented to the pilot and the navigator/WSO on the MFDs mounted in the front and rear cockpits.

Protection against air-to-air and surface-to-air missiles is ensured by electronic and infrared countermeasures equipment. The Mi-28N is fitted with a radar warning receiver and a missile warning system alerting the pilot that the helicopter is being 'painted' by enemy radars or laser target designators. This information is presented on the MFDs. Protection against heat-seeking missiles is ensured by installing chaff/flare dispensers.

The Mi-28N's armament comprises built-in cannon armament, guided missiles and unguided rockets. The NPPU-28N non-removable flexible cannon installation is fitted with the 30-mm 2A42 selectable-feed cannon (the same cannon is fitted to the Russian BMP-2 and BMP-3 infantry fighting vehicles and the BMD-2 and BMD-3 paradroppable assault fighting vehicles). The cannon installation is actuated electrically, the ammunition is belt-fed from two ammunition boxes attached to the sides of the cannon mount. This considerably enhances the cannon's reliability (there are no flexible twisting hoses). Thanks to the selective ammunition

Above and below: The starboard ESM pod housing missile warning sensors and APP-50 flare dispensers (closed by covers in this instance). The eight-pack of ATGM launch tubes is also clearly visible.

feed the crew can choose the type of rounds (armour-piercing or fragmentation/high-explosive) during the attack. Experience of the use of cannon on different versions of the Mi-24 has shown that a flexible cannon is considerably more convenient in operation: turning a four-barrel turret-mounted machine-gun on the Mi-24D takes 3 to 4 times less time than turning the whole helicopter with a fixed cannon. Besides, the helicopter fitted with a flexible cannon does not have to make a turn for hitting targets located in its rear hemisphere.

The cannon installation traverses through ±110° and moves through +13°/–40° in the vertical plane. On the Mi-28N the cannon is fired by the WSO, but the pilot can also do this with the help of the helmet-mounted sight. The cannon has a total ammunition complement of 250 rounds.

The ordnance carried externally includes:

• up to sixteen 9M120 (or 9M120F) Ataka-V, 9A2200 Vikhr' or 9M114 Shtoorm supersonic ATGMs with radio guidance systems, intended for strikes not only against ground targets but also against low-flying slow aerial targets;

• up to eight 9M39-2 Igla-V infra-red-homing air-to-air missiles;

Above and below: The second prototype Mi-28N, now with the code amended to '024 Yellow', at Zhukovskiy shortly before the MAKS-2005 airshow. Note how chipped the missile guidance radome has become. The air intake filters are enclosed by canvas covers.

Above and below: Two more views of the Mi-28N at Zhukovskiy in mid-August 2005, with some of the other exhibits (Tu-154M, Tu-204-300 and Tu-334 airliners) in the background. Note the Mil' Moscow Helicopter Plant and Rostvertol stickers on the tailboom.

Above and below: Mi-28N '0245 Yellow' makes a demonstration flight at the MAKS-2005 airshow.

Another view of the Mi-28N performing at the show. The helicopter demonstrated outstanding agility in Zhukovskiy.

• two to four B-8V20-A1 pods with 80-mm unguided rockets (20 in each pod) or B-13L1 pods with 122-mm rockets (five in each pod);

• two UPK-23-250 standardised gun pods or two KMGU-2 standardised submunitions dispensers.

The Ataka-V supersonic high-precision guided missile equipped with a radio guidance system possessing enhanced resistance to jamming is more suitable, as compared to laser guidance, for operation in smoke, dust and dense fog. The Ataka-V is capable of destroying tanks with explosive reactive armour (ERA) and low-flying slow aerial targets. The Igla-V supersonic guided missile is intended to protect the helicopter against enemy aircraft and helicopters in the 'fire-and-forget' mode. Like the cannon, the missiles of all three types are harmonised with the ammunition used by the Ground Forces of Russia. They are fired by the WSO.

The new surveillance and aiming unit ensures the detection of small-size single moving targets and group targets at a distance of several kilometres in day and night time. The ammunition includes also the S-8 and S-13 folding-fin aircraft rockets. The maximum number of FFARs that can be carried on external racks is eighty S-80s and twenty S-13s. The helicopter can also carry two UPK-23-250 standardised cannon pods with

the 23-mm GSh-23A aircraft cannon with 250 rounds for each cannon. The whole range of unguided weapons can also be operated by the pilot.

Of no small importance is the fact that the Mi-28N can be airlifted by the Ilyushin IL-76 transport aircraft with a minimum of disassembly. The designers of the helicopter claim that, as regards the cost-effectiveness criterion, the Mi-28N has no rivals at present.

In the course of several years the programme of testing the Mi-28N received practically no funding. Only thanks to the personal participation of Army General Vladimir Mikhailov, Commander-in-Chief of the Russian Air Force, did it prove possible to get things moving. In 2002 the Command of the Russian Air Force opted for the Mi-28N as the main future combat helicopter. In the following year Russian President Vladimir V. Putin issued a decree calling for the introduction of the Mi-28N into Air Force service as the main attack helicopter type. On this basis the Rost-vertol enterprise started preparations for series production of the type and laid down the initial production batch of 'Night Hunters'.

When designers embarked on development of the round-the-clock ('night-capable') version of the Mi-28 (to which the Russian military accord at present a greater degree of priority as compared to the Ka-50, in enhanc-

ing the firepower of the Russian Air Force units), they were to meet the following requirements: high flight speed, combat survivability and a very wide range of weapons. The design features of the Mi-28N reflect a balanced approach to meeting all of these requirements, albeit this has been achieved at the cost of increasing the all-up weight. However, aside from this parameter, in virtually all other respects the Mi-28N is fully on a par with its foreign counterparts. The helicopter's combat survivability has been improved by increasing the amount of armour plating, and that would be unattainable on a helicopter with a smaller AUW. At the same time the designers of the Mil' Moscow Helicopter Plant succeeded in developing a helicopter which features a relatively low radar signature.

In 2004 the Mi-28N combat helicopter's development programme underwent significant changes. Firstly, the Mil' Moscow Helicopter Plant succeeded in solving the design problems associated with developing a main gearbox compatible with the mast-mounted radar. The validity of the technical features adopted by the designers was corroborated by the 600-hour bench tests of this unit and by the 50 hours accumulated in flight on the first prototype Mi-28N (which was recoded '014 Yellow' during the trials); the work on extending the service life of the main gearbox up to

Above and below: Fresh from the Chechen theatre of operations (hence the tactical code disguised with black grease), Mi-8MTKO '29 Yellow' (c/n 94309) is seen at Zhukovskiy on 6th March 2001.

Mi-8MTKO '67 Yellow' (c/n 94691) in the static park of the MAKS-99 airshow. The GOES-321 opto-electronic 'ball turret' is clearly visible.

the target figure stipulated by the Russian MoD continues. Secondly, the first prototype Mi-28N started its flights within the framework of the joint state acceptance tests programme. Several dozen flights were performed for the purpose of evaluating the helicopter's performance and assessing the main flight limitations. In 2004 this stage of the state acceptance test was completed.

At Rostvertol, the traditional production partner of the Mil Helicopter Plant, the first pre-series (in fact, the second prototype) Mi-28N (originally coded '02 Yellow') was built while the plant was preparing for series manufacture of the type. On 25th March 2004 the machine took to the air for the first time from the factory airfield in Rostov. Six days later, on 31st March, in the presence of Russian Air Force C-in-C Vladimir S. Mikhailov, Presidential Counsellor A. G. Burootin, the leaders of Rostvertol and the Mil' Moscow Helicopter Plant, honoured guests and employees of the plant, the first pre-series Mi-28N made a demonstration flight which marked the completion of the pre-delivery tests (in fact, it was a ceremony of submitting the helicopter for manufacturer's tests). On 18th January 2005, having completed the stage of manufacturer's trials that began in March 2004, Mi-28N '02 Yellow' was ferried to the Mil' Moscow Helicopter Plant's flight test facility in Panki, south of Moscow, for the purpose of passing the ensuing stages of the joint state acceptance trials. Plans in hand envisage using the pre-series helicopter for testing the flight and navigation avionics suite and other mission equipment, for live weapons tests and for assessing the defensive equipment of the machine. To this end the helicopter is fitted with all the necessary test equipment.

On 26th May Deputy C-in-C of the Russian Air Force (Chief of Aviation) Colonel-General Aleksandr Zelin made the following statement to journalists: 'The task that we are facing is tough – the state acceptance tests of the Mi-28N shall be completed in 2005, so as to allow deliveries to the army units to begin by the end of the year'. According to Zelin, Commander in-Chief of the Russian Air Force Army General Vladimir Mikhailov 'unambiguously demanded that the industry fulfil the task thus posed with good quality and within the stipulated time'.

For a long time Rostvertol financed preparations for the production of the Mi-28N on its own. Already at the stage of the construction of the first pre-series helicopter the Rostvertol company and the subcontractor enterprises embarked on preparations for the series manufacture, and by the present time these preparations have been fully completed. When the joint state acceptance trials began, the manufacture of the main rotor blades

Above: Mi-8MTKO '67 Yellow' in flight. This was the first example of the night-capable version to be displayed publicly. Like '29 Yellow', it has triple pylons.

made of composites had been mastered. The scale of the preparatory work effected can be seen from the fact that the plant designed and manufactured more than 56,000 pieces of jigs and tools solely on the basis of funding from its own resources.

At the recent MAKS-2005 airshow in Zhukovskiy the Mil' Moscow Helicopter Plant together with Rostvertol demonstrated the first pre-series Mi-28N helicopter, which by then had the code amended to '024 Yellow'. The machine was shown both in the static park and in the flying display where it demonstrated high agility.

As early as January 2005 Russian Air Force C-in-C Army General Vladimir Mikhailov, having observed the testing of the new helicopter, stated that the Russian Ministry of Defence was going to acquire 300 Mi-24N combat helicopters. In 2006 Rostvertol must begin series manufacture of the new combat helicopters, and the first deliveries of production machines to the Russian Air Force units is planned for 2007-08. By 2010, according to Mikhailov's statement, the Russian Air Force should have 50 Mi-28N helicopters on strength.

Here it would be appropriate to note that the Russian Air Force has not finally given up on the Mi-28N's main rival – the Ka-50 single-seat combat helicopter. The proportion in which the Air Force will procure the two types (or will it?), will depend on the military and political situation – that is to say, on the spectrum of threats to Russia's national security. In all probability, both types will be purchased. Any other decision, in the opinion of Army General Mikhailov, would be tantamount to an outright squandering of the government funding, which is scant as it is.

Centre and above: Mi-8MTKO '29 Yellow' at the MAKS-2001 airshow, now with the code visible.

Above: Mi-8MTKO '205 Red', again with triple weapons pylons, is pictured under sullen skies at the MAKS-2003 airshow. It is unusual for Russian Army helicopters to have three-digit tactical codes.

Centre and above: In 2005 the Russian Air Force presented the Mi-8MTKO for the fourth time in a row at the MAKS airshows. The aircraft in question was '204 Yellow' (possibly c/n 94687).

There exists, in project form, an export version of this helicopter designated Mi-28NE (E = export). It differs insignificantly in the avionics complement.

In theory the Mi-28N, judging by its design performance and the declared capabilities of the mission avionics suite, is superior to its nearest counterpart – the Boeing (née McDonnell Douglas Helicopters) AH-64D Longbow Apache attack helicopter. The only rival of the 'Night Hunter' (again, in theory) was going to emerge in the shape of the RAH-66 Comanche, a fifth-generation reconnaissance and attack helicopter; yet, the work on this programme was terminated by the US Congress in 2004 due to the programme being too expensive. Nevertheless, paradoxically, the Mi-28N will still have to prove its advantages in the course of a long time (in the first place, the reliable work of the onboard avionics suite) not only to potential foreign customers but, first and foremost, to the Russian military, while the AH-64D has given ample proof of its combat and operational capabilities over quite some time.

Mi-8MTKO Night-Capable Transport/Assault Helicopter

Another world-famous product of the Mil' Moscow Helicopter Plant is the Mi-8 utility helicopter family, which, at the age of 44, is still going strong (the prototype first flew on 24th June 1961). The 'first-generation' Mi-8T powered by 1,500-eshp Izotov TV2-117A turboshafts soon evolved into the Mi-8MT (alias Mi-17) powered by 1,900-eshp TV3-117MT engines which first flew in 1975. Both generations have sprouted numerous specialised versions and have proved their worth more than once in armed conflicts big and small, and peacekeeping operations, in every corner of the world (except the Polar caps).

Yet, combat experience showed that the Mi-8 was handicapped by the lack of night capability, and it is mostly at night that commando groups have to be inserted/extracted. Marauding guerrilla groups likewise prefer to operate – and have to be neutralised – under the cover of darkness.

Learning from experience gained in the First Chechen War of 1994-96, the Mil' Moscow Helicopter Plant developed a night-capable version of the Mi-8MT to meet an order from the former Russian Army Aviation. (The latter does not exist as a separate service any more, as currently Russia's military rotary-wing assets are under the control of the Air Force.) Designated Mi-8MTKO, the helicopter features a GOES-320 gyrostabilised opto-electronic system (*gheerostabilizeerovannaya optiko-elektronnaya sistema*) in a very neat 'ball turret' mounted low on the starboard side of the nose. It is a product of the Urals Optomechanical Plant (UOMZ) in

Above: Mi-8MTKO '204 Yellow' arrives in Zhukovskiy to take part in the MAKS-2005 airshow. It apparently belongs to the same unit as '205 Red' shown two years earlier. This example has two external stores pylons on each side.

Yekaterinburg, the leading supplier of opto-mechanical and opto-electronic equipment to the Russian Army. The K in the designation denotes *krooglo**soo**tochnoye prime**nen**iye* (= round-the-clock capability), while the O is a reference to the opto-electronic system.

The principal mission of the Mi-8MTKO is to perform tactical reconnaissance in the interests of the ground forces, detecting small groups of the insurgents' personnel and enemy vehicles. 'Free chase' (seek and destroy) missions are also possible.

The Mi-8MTKO was publicly unveiled on 15th August 1999 when the prototype ('67 Yellow', c/n 94691) took part in the 'open doors' day at Chkalovskaya AB near Moscow, seat of the Russian Air Force's 929th State Flight Test Centre where it was undergoing trials at the time. Two days later the aircraft was displayed at the MAKS-99 airshow in Zhukovskiy (17th-22nd August 1999).

Above and below: This Mi-8MTKO in Ghelendjik in 2004 with exhaust/air mixers but no pylons bears the code '404' taped on the flightdeck blister windows. Confusingly, the air intake covers carry the c/n 94687!

The first two operational *Hip-Hs* upgraded to Mi-8MTKO standard arrived in the Chechen theatre of operations in late March 2000 (during the Second Chechen War, that is) for the purpose of evaluation in actual combat. At least one of the two was additionally equipped with a Mak-UFM (Poppy-UFM) missile warning system installed on the underside of the rear fuselage for added protection against shoulder-launched SAMs. The deployment had been ordered by the then Defence Minister of Russia Marshal Igor' S. Sergeyev.

The Mi-8MTKOs were ferried to the Chechen TO and flown in combat by test crews serving with the 344th TsBP i PLS in Torzhok. The advent of these helicopters stripped the Chechen guerrillas of their cover of darkness. However, just a few days after the deployment, on the night of 27th March 2000, one of the two choppers was lost in a crash at a mountain test range near Nal'chik,

Above: Wearing a non-standard green/brown camouflage and showing obvious signs of recoding, Mi-8MTKO '408 White' is pictured at Chkalovskaya AB. Note the 'Batman' badge indicating that this machine has seen action in Chechnya. Again, there are no external stores pylons.

Kabardino-Balkaria. The crew, consisting of Test Pilots 1st Class Lt. Col. Nikolay Kolpakov and Lt. Col. Boris Koshkin, escaped with minor injuries but the aircraft was damaged beyond repair.

The Mi-8MTKO was also in the static park at the MAKS-2001 airshow on 14th-19th August 2001 ('29 Yellow', c/n 94309) and the MAKS-2003 airshow on 19th-24th August 2002 ('205 Red', c/n unknown). The latter aircraft was apparently equipped with a different optronic system, as the 'ball turret' under the nose had a slightly different shape. A further Mi-8MTKO coded '204 Yellow' (c/n 94687?) was on display at the MAKS-2005 airshow on 16th-21st August 2005, courtesy of the Russian Air Force. '29 Yellow' was one of the examples which actually saw action in Chechnya,

and it was shown to high-ranking Russian politicians and military leaders at Zhukovskiy on 6th March 2001 shortly after returning from the Chechen theatre with the tactical code still temporarily overpainted with black grease for security reasons.

These Kazan'-built helicopters each have a single 'ball turret' on the starboard side. However, a different version of the Mi-8MTKO also exists featuring two 'ball turrets' (one on each side) and a 'thimble' radome for an ATGM guidance system supplanting the nose machine-gun mount. One such helicopter (identity unknown) saw action in Chechnya in 2001, earning the rather unkind nickname *Telepoozik* (Teletubby). (As an aside, the hideous TV show 'Teletubbies' was imported to Russia under the name 'Telepooziki' but was quickly withdrawn: those stupid characters disgusted the viewers so much that someone even created an arcade-type computer game *Kill a Teletubby*!) In February 2005, a similarly configured Ulan Ude-built Mi-8AMTSh registered 17659 (no country prefix, c/n 59489617659) and painted dark green overall was demonstrated to the Russian Federal Security Service (FSB). Subsequently this machine, now carrying no insignia whatever, was fitted out with communications intelligence (COMINT) equipment with ventral aerials for eavesdropping on the enemy and was seen at Zhukovskiy on the opening day of the MAKS-2005 airshow (16th August).

This most unusual Mi-8MTKO coded '207 Red' seen near Chkalovskaya AB has two optronic 'ball turrets', a Kontoor weather radar, plus a triangular aerial atop the tailboom and and a ventral dielectric fairing of unknown purpose (these are probably associated with signals intelligence).

Two more views of the same helicopter, propped up on hydraulic jacks. This is a late-production Kazan'-built example with a Mi-8MTV-5 style extra entry door to starboard (hence the high position of the KO-50 cabin heater). Note the additional flightdeck and engine bay armour and the ventral moveable searchlight.

Left: One of the famous 'Teletubbies' taking off with four-packs of anti-tank guided missiles on the outer pylons. One of the 'ball turrets' under the nose is associated with missile guidance, as is the thimble radome just visible at the tip of the nose.

Right: Another 'Teletubby' – this time an overall green Mi-8AMTSh operated by one of the Russian security agencies in a communications intelligence role.

Below right: Another view of the SIGINT-configured Mi-8AMTSh at Zhukovskiy; note the ventral antenna farm and the total lack of markings.

Below: Mi-8MTKO '27 Yellow' displays a non-standard camouflage scheme.

Above and below: Two more views of the unmarked COMINT helicopter as it takes off at Zhukovskiy in August 2005.

Chapter 6

Kamovs in Combat

In late 2000, at the height of the Second Chechen War, the Russian newspapers and magazines started running headlines like *'Black Sharks' in Chechnya*. The story of the Kamov Ka-50 attack helicopter's baptism of fire calls for some explanation.

Despite its plans to order large quantities of the Mil' Mi-28N Night Hunter attack helicopter as a replacement for the long-serving Mi-24, the Russian Air Force has not given up its plans to field the competing Ka-50 Black Shark and its two-seat derivative, the Ka-52 Alligator, in limited numbers. All the more so since the Ka-50 had been declared the winner of the fly-off with the Mi-28 and, upon completion of its state acceptance trials, had been officially included in the Russian Army Aviation inventory by Presidential decree on 25th August 1995.

When the First Chechen War began in December 1994, voices were heard urging that the Russian Army should use its latest hardware – the Ka-50 – against the bandits; in the popular press and at the *Svoboda slova* (Freedom of Speech) talk show the public urged to 'get a few Black Sharks in there and give 'em hell'. Apparently the Russian Ministry of Defence supported the idea of testing the Ka-50 in its proper element. Hence in 1995 a decision was taken to form an Experimental Combat Detachment (ECD) comprising four Ka-50s and four Ka-29 assault/transport helicopters converted into reconnaissance/target spotting helicopters for operational trials on the Chechen theatre of operations.

One of the men behind the MoD's decision was Maj. Gen. Boris A. Vorob'yov, holder of the Hero of Russia title and Commander of the Russian Army Aviation's 344th Combat & Conversion Training Centre (TsBP i PLS) in the town of Torzhok. Tragically, Vorob'yov was later killed in the crash of a pre-production Ka-50 ('021 White outline') at the Centre's airfield on 17th June 1998. In 1995 appropriate orders were given to earmark four Ka-50s and two Ka-29s for the newly formed ECD; two more Ka-29s were to follow later.

Shortly afterwards the Kamov Co. started preparing two initial-production Ka-50s coded '22 Yellow' and '24 Yellow' for the Chechen tour. One of the helicopters had been manufactured by the 'Progress' Arsen'yev Aircraft Production Association (AAPO) in the Russian Far East (reportedly c/n 3538054301099 and f/n 0304), while the other machine had been built by the company's own experimental production facility in Ukhtomskaya near Moscow. For security reasons both helicopters had the tactical codes removed for the duration, therefore it is not known which one is which. The modifications included installation of a missile warning system with sensor blisters on the forward and rear fuselage sides to alert the pilot that the helicopter was being illuminated by a laser ranger/target designator.

Concurrently work went ahead on two Ka-29s. The first of these, a company demonstrator coded '38 Yellow' (c/n 17811), was equipped with the same 2A42 selectable-feed 30-mm cannon as fitted to the Ka-50; additionally, a special targeting and communications suite called KSAS (*kompleks sredstv avtomatizahtsiï i svyazi* – automation and comms suite) was installed to improve navigational and target spotting accuracy and enable secure communications. The other machine ('35 Yellow'), which received attention a while later, had the KSAS suite and the Rubikon flight/navigation/attack suite as fitted to the Ka-50. Additionally, for protection against heat-seeking shoulder-launched anti-aircraft missiles the Ka-29s were fitted with decoy flare dispensers on the fuselage sides and Ka-50 style air/exhaust mixers on the engine jetpipes. Both modified helicopters bore the designation Ka-29VPNTsU (*vozdooshnyy poonkt navedeniya i tsele'ookazahniya* – airborne guidance and target designation post).

Ka-50 '25 Yellow' (c/n 8798000025), showing the location of the MWS sensors and the exhaust/air mixers reducing the helicopter's heat signature.

Above: The cockpit of the same helicopter, showing the display of the Rubikon flight/nav/attack suite and the red ejection handles of the K-37 ejection seat.

A while later two more initial-production Ka-50s operated by the 344th TsBP i PLS – '20 Yellow' (c/n 3538053302030) and '21 Yellow' (c/n 3538052402045) – were ferried to the Kamov Company's test facility for modification. The conversion of the first two Ka-50s had been financed by Kamov; now, however, the company was unable to pay for the modification of two more machines and the second pair of Black Sharks was stuck at Ukhtomskaya, missing the tour.

In the meantime, the First Chechen War had ended with the Khasavyurt peace accord of 1996. In 1997 the upgraded Ka-50s and Ka-29s returned to Torzhok where their improved combat efficiency was confirmed in the course of a tactical exercise.

After the war, the Russian MoD concentrated on eliminating the deficiencies in the weaponry and training of the ground forces which had borne the brunt of the campaign. Thus, when the Second Chechen War broke out in August 1999 with the guerrillas' invasion of Daghestan, on 29th November that year the MoD decided to form a Combat Strike Group (CSG) consisting of two Ka-50s and a single Ka-29VPNTsU for use in such 'hot spots'.

By then the 344th TsBP i PLS had only one upgraded Ka-50 ('24 Yellow') available. Therefore the Kamov Co. decided to modify the fifth prototype Ka-50 coded '25 Yellow' (formerly '015 Yellow', c/n 8798000025) for inclusion into the CSG. In keeping with the Army Aviation's instructions the helicopters were fitted with bulletproof side windows and additional armour protection for the cockpit floor; moreover, the avionics suite was augmented by the KABRIS data processing/display system which generated an electronic

map allowing the pilot to navigate to the target with an error margin of just a few dozen metres.

In the course of eight months (December 1999 to July 2000) the two modified Ka-50s and the Ka-29VPNTsU made more than 150 test flights, the Black Sharks accounting for 125 of these. The operational techniques of working with the target spotter chopper and forward area control using a man-portable KSAS computerised control console were developed at this stage.

In December 2000 the CSG finally redeployed to the North Caucasian TO, operating from Khankala AB near the Chechen capital of Groznyy. The newly-arrived helicopter pilots were unfamiliar with the area they would have to fly and fight in, so they were given familiarisation flights in Mi-24s. Shortly afterwards the Black Sharks finally began flying actual combat sorties; these were flown by either mixed pairs (a Ka-50 and a Mi-24) or by both Ka-50s accompanied by the Ka-29VPNTsU. On 6th January 2001, as Ka-50 '25 Yellow' was making an ultra-low-level attack against a target designated by the Ka-29, the pilot sensed abnormal vibration after completing the firing pass and elected to make a precautionary landing at Khankala. Post-flight inspection revealed nothing more serious than a damaged blade tip; after repairs the helicopter returned to active duty.

By 14th February 2001 the CSG choppers and the escorting Mi-24s had made 121 sorties totalling more than 110 hours; of these, 76 sorties with a total duration of more than 63 hours were flown by the contra-rotating Kamovs. One of the main outcomes of this brief deployment was incontovertible proof that the Rubikon automated flight/navigation/attack suite considerably eased the pilot workload during single-pilot combat helicopter operations. The Chechen tour of duty had demonstrated that, despite their limited experience with the Ka-50, the pilots of the CSG were quick to master the contra-rotating chopper with all its peculiarities. The Rubikon suite allowed the Ka-50 to bring all of its weapons to bear on the target in a single firing pass. The KABRIS system also proved its worth; the digital map allowed the pilot to see both his own position and that of other helicopters in the group relative to the designated targets. The CSG's commander stated later that, once very minor modifications had been made to the helicopter, an average Air Force pilot would be able to make an instrument landing in the Ka-50 with no ground visibility, relying solely on the information provided by the KABRIS. Another important result of the Chechen tour was that the Ka-50 had demonstrated its high reliability during intensive combat operations; no serious malfunctions were recorded.

Ka-29VPNTsU '35 Yellow' at the Kamov Co.'s new test facility at Chkalovskaya AB. Note the sensor window of the Rubikon suite, the flare dispensers (closed by red covers) and the Ka-50 style exhaust/air mixers.

Above: The production line in Arsen'yev, with at least ten unfinished Ka-50s waiting for funds to be allocated for their completion.

The pilots who flew the Ka-50 in combat recommended that certain changes be made to the placement of the information displays in the helicopter's cockpit and to the data presentation modes. Other recommendations concerned the introduction of thermal imaging systems enabling night operations, changes in the operating algorithm of the decoy flare dispensers and the introduction of a fully capable electronic support measures (radar/missile warning) suite. Generally, however, the results of the Ka-50/Ka-29VPNTsU group's combat debut were deemed satisfactory.

The persistent financial troubles afflicting Russia in the 1990s (including the 1998 bank crisis) and the resulting stoppage of new military aircraft procurement by the Russian MoD mean that the Ka-50, despite being officially on the inventory, still has not entered service in any significant numbers. By 2004 AAPO 'Progress' had managed to complete and deliver a mere nine Ka-50s, with about a dozen more airframes minus engines and avionics waiting their turn at the plant. Some of these nine helicopters are in service with the 344th TsBP i PLS, the remainder being used by the Kamov Co. for test and development purposes.

With no funding forthcoming, the AAPO production line stood still for several years, the helicopters gathering dust in the final assembly shop. However, in 2005 Radio Lemma (one of the local radio stations in the

Russian Far East) broadcast encouraging news; following a motion by People's Deputy (= Member of Parliament) Vitaliy Grishookov, the Security Council of the Russian State Duma (Parliament) took up the issue of Ka-50/Ka-52 series production and filed a formal query to the Ministry of Defence. The latter responded that plans are in hand to finance the completion of five more Ka-50s in 2005-06. The plans also envisaged the completion of the Ka-52's state acceptance trials which have been suspended because of the programme's uncertain status; this would allow the government's defence order book

and the State defence programme for 2006-2015 to be suitably amended.

In late March 2004 Presidential advisor Aleksandr Burootin paid a visit to AAPO 'Progress', examining the production line and assessing the possibilities of the unfinished Ka-50s being completed (as well as of Ka-52 production being launched). This event spelled hope for the plant; after several years of oblivion the Ka-50 programme seemed to be coming in from the cold at last. Yet, in a sort of mockery at the plant's name, no real progress has been made since the famous visit; the assembly shops are as quiet as ever.

'061 White outline', the Ka-52 prototype, in its latest configuration with a mast-mounted radar, dorsal and ventral sensor turrets and a dielectric nose.

Red Star Volume 19
SOVIET HEAVY INTERCEPTORS

Yefim Gordon

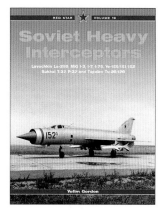

In the nervous 1950s, the Soviet Union faced the task of defending its borders against intrusions by Western spyplanes or bomber attacks. Aircraft developed for this priority long-range interception task included Mikoyan's I-3, I-7U, I-75 and Ye-152 which paved the way for the MiG-25, Sukhoi's T-37, terminated before it had a chance to fly, and Tupolev's Tu-128 – so huge it was mistaken for a medium bomber in the West.

Softback, 280 x 215 mm, 128 pages
159 b/w photos, 12pp of colour,
plus 23pp of line drawings
1 85780 191 1 **£18.99**

Red Star Volume 20
SOVIET/RUSSIAN UNMANNED AERIAL VEHICLES

Yefim Gordon

The Lavochkin OKB's La-17, produced in target drone and recce versions, was the first Soviet UAV to find large-scale use. The Tupolev OKB also developed a line of UAVs, including the Tu-123 Yastreb, Tu-141 Strizh, Tu-243 Reys and the latest Tu-300 recce/strike UAV. Yakovlev's unmanned aircraft are also covered including the Pchela (Bee) surveillance UAV. Mention is also made of UAVs and drones developed by such companies as Strela and the Moscow Aviation Institute.

Softback, 280 x 215 mm, 128 pages
143 b/w photos, 29pp of colour,
plus line drawings
1 85780 193 8 **£18.99**

Red Star Volume 21
ANTONOV'S JET TWINS
The An-72/-74 Family

Yefim Gordon and Dmitriy Komissarov

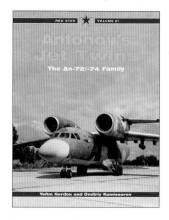

The need to provide a state-of-the-art jet successor to the An-26 led Antonov to develop a twin-turbofan tactical airlifter, the An-72, with its signature high-mounted engines, employing the Coanda effect to dramatically improve wing lift and STOL capability.

The prototype flew in 1977 but it was not until the mid-1980s that production began. Comprehensive listings, both of An-72s and An-74s, detail registration/ Bort number, c/n, f/n and operator.

Softback, 280 x 215 mm, 128 pages
125 colour, 90 b/w photographs,
4pp of line drawings
1 85780 199 7 **£19.99**

Red Star Volume 22
MIL'S HEAVYLIFT HELICOPTERS

Y Gordon, S & D Komissarov

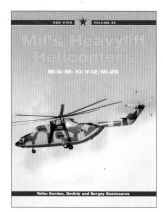

The prototype Mil' Mi-6 heavy transport and assault helicopter first flew in 1957. In 1959 it served as the basis for the unconventional Mi-10. In 1967, Mil' amazed the world with the mighty V-12 capable of lifting a 25-ton payload; then in 1977 the OKB achieved success with the smaller but more advanced Mi-26, the world's largest production helicopter. The development history, design and civil and military use of all three types is described in detail.

Softback, 280 x 215 mm, 128 pages
174 b/w photographs, 21pp of colour,
10pp of line drawings
1 85780 206 3 **£19.99**

Red Star Volume 23
SOVIET/RUSSIAN AWACS AIRCRAFT

Yefim Gordon and Dmitriy Komissarov

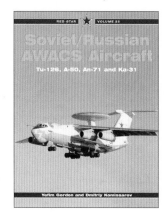

The need for effective protection of Soviet airspace in areas lacking adequate cover by ground radars led to work on airborne early warning systems. The Tu-126 AEW aircraft, evolved from the Tu-114 airliner, entered service in 1961. It was replaced in the early 1980s by the Ilyushin/Beriyev A-50 AWACS based on the IL-76MD. The highly unorthodox An-71 with its tail-mounted rotodome and the Ka-31 AEW helicopter are also described plus other unbuilt projects.

Softback, 280 x 215 mm, 128 pages
144 colour, 70 b/w photographs,
plus 5pp of line drawings
1 85780 215 2 **£19.99**

Red Star Volume 24
TUPOLEV Tu-144
Russia's Concorde

Yefim Gordon and Vladimir Rigmant

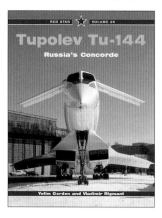

Tasked with creating a supersonic transport ahead of the West as a matter of national prestige, Andrey Tupolev met the target at the cost of a tremendous research and development effort. The Tu-144 took to the air in December 1968, ahead of the Anglo-French Concorde. This detailed account includes the reasons behind its premature withdrawal and a description of its recent use in a joint research programme with NASA.

Softback, 280 x 215 mm, 128 pages
151 b/w photos, 15 pages of colour
plus drawings
1 85780 216 0 **£19.99**

Red Star Volume 25
ILYUSHIN IL-12 & IL-14
Successors to the Li-2

Yefim Gordon and Dmitry Komissarov

Designed to supersede the Li-2, the 29-seat IL-12 airliner entered Aeroflot service in 1948. Some 600 were built for Aeroflot and the Soviet armed forces. The improved IL-14 entered production in 1953, the type was exported to China, Bulgaria, Romania and Poland as well as being built by VEB in East Germany and Asia in Czechoslovakia. The total production of over 1,000 aircraft included 203 Avia 14s and Avia 14 Supers – the latter being a pressurised development.

Softback, 280 x 215 mm, 128 pages
180 b/w photos, 16 pages of colour
plus 12 pages of drawings
1 85780 223 3 **£19.99**